Richard Bollman, SJ
SELECTED HOMILIES

allowing life experience to open up
the ways and the Word of God

Selected Homilies: allowing life experience to open up the ways and the Word of God
Copyright 2019 by Richard Bollman, SJ & VITALITY Cincinnati, Inc.,
Published by VITALITY Cincinnati, Inc. (U.S.A.)
vitalitycincinnati.org

This book has been published to raise funds for VITALITY Cincinnati, a 501(c)3 education-based nonprofit. All proceeds from sales of this book benefit the mission of VITALITY Cincinnati: sharing holistic self-care from neighborhood to neighborhood, person to person, and breath by breath since 2010.

All rights reserved. No part of this book may be reproduced in any form or by any means, electronic or mechanical, without written permission of the author or VITALITY Cincinnati's Board of Trustees. The author and VITALITY Cincinnati grant that brief quotations of seven lines or less from this book may be used when the full title and full authorship contained on the book cover is named.

The opinions and ideas expressed herein are those of the author and do not necessarily represent the opinions of the Board of Trustees of VITALITY Cincinnati. Any errors, of course, are solely the author's.

Every effort has been made to give credit to other people's original ideas through the text itself and acknowledgments that follow this text. If you feel something should be credited to someone and is not, please get in touch through vitalitycincinnati.org and every effort will be made to correct this text for future printings. Thank you!

We invite you to honor your mind, your body, your whole self. Do only what you know to be right for you. While the invitations offered here in this book, on VITALITY's website and social media, and in our classes are geared to be gentle and easily modified by the participant to fit the participants's needs, please consult your medical doctor or health professional before undertaking any practices shared by VITALITY, its staff, or volunteers.

Doug Klocke of Klocke Design created the book cover and interior images.
Julie Lucas of withinwonder.com created VITALITY's logos.

ISBN: 978-145757-017-9
Library of Congress Control Number: 2019912127

**in gratitude to our VATRONS
who seek with us all a new way forward &
who have helped bring forward this new book
by contributing $25 or more to make this publication possible**

we thank you!

Anonymous, Sandy Bachman, JL Baralt Burkhart
Jeanne & Chris Barnes, Stephanie & Phillip Beck Borden
Georgeanne & Jim Bender, James Binder, Kathleen Blieszner & Jerome Glinka
Christopher Bolling & Stephen Peterson, Karen Brandstetter & Patrick Cusick
Marisa & Will Brandstetter & Charles Hunter, Helen Buswinka, Nora Buzek
Joyce & Tom Choquette, Beauly & Jim Cira, Mary Koenig-Clapp & David Clapp
Peg & Joe Conway, Raven & John Crawford-Dunn
Mary Tighe Cronin & Timothy Cronin, Cindy Crown & Dave Flaspohler
Barb Dardy, Ronda Deel, Lois & Charles Deitschel
Flo & Tom DeWitt, Mary Dickerson, Ruth Ann & Jim Doerger
Mary Duennes, Judy Evans, Susan & Howard Fahrmeier
Sally Fellerhoff, Dottie Fields & Bill Klykylo, Bonnie Finn
Jane & Bob Friel, The Gahl Family, Marge & Neil Gambow
Michele & Chris Geiger, Tom Green, Pat Greulich, Ursula Hassell
Ed Hausfeld, Chris & John Heatherman, Katherine Heile
Chris & Steve Hils, Susan Hochbein, Kristen & John Hundemer
Mary Hurlburt, Robert Jablonski, Jannette & Mike Jarrold-Grapes
Jill Johnson, Joyce Kahle CPPS, Barb Kelly, Joyce Kelly
Rachel & Matt Kemper, Jean & Jack Kennevan, Liz Keuffer
Doug Klocke & Tom Freeman, Mary Kay & Louis Kroner
Maria Krzeski, Marilyn & Charles Kuntz, The Lewandowski Family
Todd Long, Robert Lorsbach, Annette Lucker, Allie & George Maggini
Kathy & Tim McGrath, Mary Beth & Ed Muntel, Julie M Murray
Kathleen Murray, Peg & Fran Niehaus, Mary O'Dwyer, Nancy & Jim Ollier
Andrea & Rogers O'Neill, Sally Neidhard, Jenny & Ed Ostendorf
Barbara & Butch Otting, Bonnie & Dick Peterson, Daniel Pfahl
Ann Plyer, Margaret Quinn, Pat Reaman, Mary Anne Reese
Fran Repka RSM, Judy Reinhold, Leah & Sean Reynolds
Kathy & Tom Riga, Susan Russell, Amy Schardein
Pat & Sam Schloemer, Mary & Bob Schneider, Lucy Schultz
Bob Seery, Anne Schoelwer & Steve Lavelle, Brian Shircliff
Velda Smiley & Paul Schulte, Peggy & Karl Smith, Donna Lynn Smyth
Frank Spataro, Ruth Steinert Foote & Roger Foote, Cindy Stiens
Nancy Strapp, Jean Marie Stross & Daniel Price
The Strunks, Elaine Suess & Janet Montgomery, Joy & Bob Thaler
Patrice Trauth, Jude & Ed Vonderbrink, Sam & Gerry Weller
Trisha & Mike Wendling, Linda Wheeler, Amy & Steve Whitlatch
Connie Widmer, Linda Wihl, Sue Wilke, Carol D & Lee Yeazell
Carol T & Bruce Yeazell, Linda & Jim Young

In gratitude for permission to quote from these works . . .

Scripture texts in this work are taken from the New American Bible, revised edition © 2010, 1991, 1986, 1970 Confraternity of Christian Doctrine, Washington, D.C. and are used by permission of the copyright owner. All Rights Reserved. No part of the New American Bible may be reproduced in any form without permission in writing from the copyright owner. All of these Scripture texts in this book have been printed in **bold-italic** type.

"Gott spricht zu jedem.../God speaks to each of us..." from RILKE'S BOOK OF HOURS: LOVE POEMS TO GOD by Rainer Maria Rilke, translated by Anita Barrows and Joanna Macy, translation copyright © 1996 by Anita Barrows and Joanna Macy. Used by permission of Riverhead, an imprint of Penguin Publishing Group, a division of Penguin Random House LLC. All rights reserved.

The Wisdom Jesus, by Cynthia Bourgeault, © 2008. Reprinted by arrangement with Shambhala Publications, Inc., Boulder, CO. www.shambhala.com.

Tikkun by Rabbi Michael Lerner www.tikkun.org.

a small portion of Ludolph of Saxony's Vita Christi as published in *Studies in the Spirituality of Jesuits*, Spring 2011, p. 25. "The Prologue of Ludolph's Vita Christi," commentary and translation by Milton Walsh . . . recently expanded *Ludolph of Saxony, Carthusian. The Life of Jesus Christ, Part One.* Vol. 1, Chapters 1-40. Translated and Introduced by Milton T. Walsh. Collegeville, MN: Liturgical Press, 2018. Cistercian Studies Series: Two Hundred Sixty-Seven.

Barbara Fiand, Bellarmine parishioner, gave me permission to quote from her book *In the Stillness You Will Know*, Crossroad Publishing, 2002, p. 58.

CONTENTS

BACK STORY 1

1. OPENING THE WORD 5
　meeting places
　you have the treasure
　finding your church
　the comfort of time
　the narrow doors

2. THE ADVENT OF GOD 25
　the waking time
　winter welcome
　the wilderness road
　a river of repentance
　the reed not shaken
　risking encounter
　in the company of Mary

3. STORIES OF CHRISTMAS 50
　longing for home
　all you can buyw
　a Christmas visitor
　this night in Bethlehem
　the new birth
　the grace of the big bang
　the story of Herod
　consider the magi

4. MEETING JESUS 85
　who he is
　knowing what to do

    salt and light
    invitations
    learning to follow
    trusting the one you know

5. THE PASCHAL STORY 111
    giving up
    finding yourself
    learning to see
    the raising of Lazarus 1
    the raising of Lazarus 2
    the raising of Lazarus 3
    the world is not the way it has to be
    toward emmaus
    Christ hidden among us

6. DISCIPLESHIP 148
    martha's house
    there will be enough
    getting closer to see
    sent to be yourself
    what's on our plates?
    reaching past divisions
    talking about love
    a call worth trusting

7. END TIME 181
    the nearness of God
    together in hope
    paradise within
    in remembrance of her
    the one we wait for

8. THANKSGIVING 200
    a national story
    a personal story

ACKNOWLEDGMENTS 209

BACK STORY

Shortly after I was ordained, I began a graduate program in English Literature at the State University of New York in Buffalo. This was the early Seventies, an era when many English departments were asserting themselves in multi-disciplinary conversations about culture, politics, psyche and science. My short history as a priest, fresh from theology studies in the wake of Vatican II, made me welcome enough in the mix, closer in age to my professors than the other grad students, with a related field of study and a lore of scriptural references that stood me well in the early centuries of poetry. Courses were set up to prod the official canon of literature to see how it actually worked in its own era, and brought help or challenge to ours. I recall being invited to roam the pastoral woods of Elizabethan poetry with the mind of the Viet Cong.

At the same time I looked for community in faith, following a need to keep making sense of my Christian and Jesuit roots. To some extent this was a search for a secure identity now that seminary life was over. What is my work, who do I connect to, what do I feel as a man and a human being that can give me direction toward God, how do I recognize my own sacred story? And clearly, the important truth I found is that I was not alone with these hopes and questions. A community of families had already formed on the campus of the Jesuit college where I lived, an alternative parish of sorts, and they took me in! I was one of three clergy who chose to worship there in the student center basement on Sunday mornings, welcome to preside and preach in rotation.

The following year, a community of religious women founded a House of Prayer, drawn from several congregations in the city: teachers, health-care workers, some retired, some new to religious life. They became a weekday community for me and another priest from the diocese, a call to begin my Tuesdays and Thursdays at 6:30 a.m., whether rain or snow or clear cold skies. It's as if here too, with the lay Catholic world and the Sisters' communities, the life of traditional prayer was mixed with a conversation about culture, politics, justice, family, psyche and soul. So it was that early on in my life as a priest I was blessed with people around me who loved stories, poems, words, and the Word, and who welcomed me, with them, not only to take heart, but to find voice, to join the conversation that speaks about God. What do we talk about when we want to venture into those matters? It was more than a preacher's dilemma, it was a common need.

I had the good luck to be offered a teaching position in English literature at the University of San Francisco. This was 1974. Northern California was at the time alive with conversations about God, from Big Sur in the south, to Mount Shasta and the Trappist monasteries in the north, a time of summer schools and workshops, dialogue with Asian traditions, the human potential movement, revolutionary politics, and the first decade of passage across old Christian boundaries initiated by the second Vatican Council. It was easy to get hooked in, and to find the Christian community avidly involved ("oh, you're Catholic too!"). So while I tried to remain focused on the beginning of a teaching career, I kept finding not only alternate paths of spirituality but other ways of learning, other things we should be talking about.

On a Catholic campus I had the chance to stay at work on sermons. They became for me moments of remembered dialogue with friends, teachers, guides, students. They were times of trying to sort out what mattered most to me, something I couldn't quite do in my chosen profession and still create a viable argument for tenure. Indeed my application was denied, and then taken up in a grievance process by our new faculty union. An argument was made, and even accepted, that were I to submit twelve sermon texts I'd be presenting a publication, with an actual audience, at least as broad as a small poetry volume. I submitted the twelve sermons and secured my job. But another offer made more immediate sense to me.

When I left academic life for pastoral ministry at the Jesuit spirituality center in Milford, and eventually service as pastor at Bellarmine Chapel in Cincinnati, one student unforgettably said she saw why the change called out to me. "Now you can work directly with the themes you always want to get around to in English class." She had it right. As a teacher I had an almost naive obsession with the truth poets told, the truth of faith or doubt, what we could take from them for our own consolation or challenge. How can Herbert, even Milton, work toward the transformation of the reader, set out some traces of the journey we were all making. It's an almost eccentric point of view in academe, but it fit in nicely at a retreat house.

Richard Bollman, SJ

Preaching remains for me a weekly insistent purpose, an event of public speaking where, at its best, you find the "Amen" that a congregation offers with its nods, laughter, eyes that take in or question, silence which carries words to where they can settle in and be fruitful. It's an open project. We're all involved. I have left these homilies in the form of spoken lines, reminding you that they are spoken events. They follow the order of the liturgical cycle from November to November, which itself has a kind of rambling parallel to an Ignatian retreat, connected to the scriptures of a year, with sidebars of world events, local struggles, and anniversaries. Though they might accumulate meaning in thematic groups, I think they make the best sense one at a time. They are offered as part of the dialogue we've been living, and continue to live in this demanding, transformative time.

Selected Homilies

1. OPENING THE WORD

In all the words we hear or read, we listen for "the Word." In chance encounters, prayer meetings, news events, a novel maybe or a movie, you keep listening. We trust God to be there, to speak up, to touch us "in person" and "directly," as Ignatius Loyola says at the start of his Spiritual Exercises. All of it has a way of interacting with the Sunday scripture. The following small set of homilies are a kind of random demonstration of how the discovered Word arises from a chance conversation or a public event

meeting places

Feast Day of St. John Lateran Basilica
September 9, 1978
University of San Francisco

Then he brought me back to the entrance of the temple, and there! I saw water flowing out from under the threshold of the temple toward the east. He said to me, "This water flows out into the eastern district. Wherever it flows, the river teems with every kind of living creature; fish will abound. Where these waters flow they refresh; everything lives where the river goes." (Ezekiel 47:1, 8a, 9)

His disciples recalled the words of scripture,
"Zeal for your house will consume me." (John 2:17)

HOMILY

There was a particularly fine sunrise this morning.
Just enough haze and industrial smoke curled against the Oakland hills
to catch the light and intensify its color
against an unusually clear upper sky.
A silver planet burned high above the horizon
till the sun showed itself, all white and gold,
and the planet melted away. And at that same moment
it became impossible anymore to watch the sun directly,
but the grass and trees, the window glass of distant buildings,
everything was catching its glory.

I'm not often awake to see the sunrise,
but I'm glad I saw one this morning.
Ezekiel, who loved Jerusalem, would often have seen
the procession of the sun turning the city gold,
its light streaming into the eastern gate of the Temple.
The "glory of God" he called it once,
brightening every object
and filling every corner of the city and the temple court,
warm, powerful, dazzling, inescapable–
this is what the image conveys about the true God.
And in the passage today, Ezekiel is intent on what he hears,
something gradually more clear, like rushing water,
that became a word, an utterance from the heart of God
to the heart of his prophet.
"Yes, I am here, powerful for life, pervasive,
and I mean to remain here.
And this Temple is the sacred source.
Let it fill you up."

We hear about Ezekiel and the Temple today
because in Rome, our own holy city, there is commemorated
the dedication centuries ago of the Church of St. John Lateran,
a sacred place, preceding even St. Peter's in time and importance.
It was the first cathedral for the bishop of Rome,

Richard Bollman, SJ

given by the Lateran family, and the Pope is its pastor.
I do not know whether its door faces east, though it probably does.
I actually walked through the place
on a rather rapid tour of the city, and I remember its baroque, pillared facade,
and the rows of columns inside, the upper story of windows.
But it is not necessary to picture what St. John Lateran looks like,
or to know its origins and several previous structures.
Today's occasion asks rather that we remember our own sacred places:
this church itself, with its own columns and upper windows,
all this color in the morning sun right now,
or the churches of our past, or chapels, or homes,
groves of trees or seashores.
All of them—Temples of divine Presence.

I remember speaking with a young woman,
a student new to the campus here, not a Catholic:
I forget her precise church affiliation.
She described her first visit to this church.
She said that she had for several years been unable to find God in churches.
They seemed to her too conventional and drab, so standard and cold.
But the mere size of this church from outside impressed her
and it dawned on her that she should give it a try.

"So," she said, "I went in, out of curiosity to see if God lived there.
And," she said, "he does." I was relieved.
She said it had something to do with size and silence
and the beauty of the light,
that it was clear to her God was there, and she spoke to him.

You might think her naive or confused, but she certainly was telling the truth,
the same way Ezekiel told the truth when he was so aware of God's presence
and God's rushing life in the temple, that he fell prone.
My student friend was speaking for herself,
but Ezekiel spoke for a whole people.
But they both claimed the same thing: they had found God,
they had listened to something beyond words.
The good news is this: God lives on earth.

Selected Homilies

He has a local habitation: he resides like light,
he speaks in great silent spaces and deep waters.

It is a useful question to ask yourself,
where have you found God; where does he live for you,
where has he shown up even unexpectedly?
What places are sacred to you for the hope and light they have held?
Are you a person with a history of meetings with God?
Are they long past, or do they continue?
Is the temple of his presence now in ruins, or is it lost to you,
or are you for the first time looking for it?
What naive questions.
For our better mind knows that God is everywhere, and invisible.
But still we are human people with a finite history,
physical senses and imagination:
events, places, people, form the occasions where God might show up,
the temple for us, the gathering of light we saw,
one picnic afternoon on a Pacific slope when everybody's voice fell silent.
Or the voice we really hear under everything,
maybe even here in this church, underneath our mental chatter,
in the pulse of our breathing. "Trust me," it says,
and you plunge in for just awhile.

Give some thought this day to your own history of places.
It's not messages we need to remember, but presence.
We can recall where where we've been. Even now you find places
crowding up in your imagination, I'll bet. They are very likely
the right ones, speaking to you.
Do this as we remember that centuries ago a church was dedicated,
the first in Rome to hold our collective story.
In this larger chronicle of temples and basilicas
your story takes its own importance. Trust it.

And then let me add this too.
Why was that place holy?
Why did God show himself, hint at himself,
speak quietly in the silence,
why did he open the door of presence there, for you?

Richard Bollman, SJ

Was it because the fretwork in the arches was especially fine,
or the trees fragrant or the rushing stream powerful?
Was it because the haze was perfect against the Oakland hills,
or a silver planet still gleamed above the horizon?
Or, what I believe, what we hear this morning,
God was there because you were there.
He entered in because your door was open.
For you were God's temple then, and still are,
the temple of his presence, bone and muscle and heart.
You have been made as a dwelling place for him.
This grand church is here only to remind you
of the beauty and sacredness of your life.
Every week you make your way to this place here on Parker and Fulton.
So just as often, make your way to the temple of your heart.
Nothing is needed: no great sacrificial act, no burnt offering.
All that has been accomplished.
Let the zeal of the Lord himself clear away
the extra traffic and business there,
turn over all the tables, cast out all the useless effort
by which you hope to win God to your side.
God is already at your side, on your side.
Breathe easily. Open your senses. The word is silent. Gratitude.

you have the treasure

17th Sunday, A
Romans 8:28-34; Matthew 13:44-46

Today's Gospel concludes the sermon of Parables in Matthew. These two parables support one another, evoking the Kingdom of Heaven, which is Matthew's way of saying the Kingdom of God. It is what you really want: this field, this pearl.

Selected Homilies

And then in Paul's letter, the apostle announces how God has a desire to bless each of us and to enrich us with spirit. Not just prophets and kings, but ourselves too: The word of God is full of promise.

HOMILY

A few days ago I had a conversation with a young black man.
We met at a local hospital waiting for some coffee
at one of these little cafes in the corridors they have.
There weren't many open tables, so we shared one,
and it was easy to just start talking.
This man had such an open and happy face.
Maybe forty years old, and a long set of dreadlocks. I couldn't look away.

It turns out he works at the hospital, which explained maybe the tie he wore,
and the jacket. He helps to run a group in the psychiatric unit.
It's part of a training program he's in, toward accreditation as a counselor.
"You seem to like what you do," I said, and he smiled, kind of shrugged,
and said, "Well I fit in up there. You might say I'm a graduate."
Yes, it turns out he had gone through the ordeal of an early mental illness,
and learned how to deal with it, to understand things gradually,
to remember to take his meds, and, he added, "to just be grateful."

So I said, well, yes, "grateful to be healthy, to have your life back."
"More than that," he said. "I'm just grateful to be human. A human being.
I have this meditation practice, nothing much, but mainly gratitude,
and feeling myself to be human, my body, my mind, you know?"
He spoke with the joy of a man who has found something.

Okay, I'm summing things up, but this was a real conversation,
I can see him now, and what I said to him next is the honest truth.
I told him I have this church job, and I need to talk on Sunday,
and we have this part of the Bible that says: "We know
that all things work for good for those who love God."

Richard Bollman, SJ

Does that make sense for you? I asked him that. And he said,
"Love, that's what it is, I can say that . . . (and he went on,)
Is it God? Not God as he used to be, somebody you picture or look for,
but just a presence, bigger than that old God, just here."
So I had been talking with someone who loves God. You never know.
He was a kind of insider.

Jesus too would talk about God, the Kingdom of heaven,
the realm of God, which is to say God's place,
God's presence and connection with us,
and when you get a feel for it, it's like finding something,
a treasure that had been buried,
and what you want is to have access to that treasure.

I think of the young man working at the hospital, finding a way
to be close to life, close to spirit, in gratitude, in loving people.
Finding a pearl that is beyond any other thing you've seen,
new and precious and you want to claim it.
Not because you want to be wealthy, but because
you want to be close to what really matters, to what you value.
This is a way of respecting the parable today: the field, the pearl.
What you value.

But then, to get there, to the treasure, the pearl, I'm thinking now,
we need to sell all the extra stuff, all we don't need,
for the sake of having what we really desire.
I had the feeling, talking with the man at the hospital,
that recovery from mental illness took a lot of patience and sacrifice for him,
coming up to be honest, to trust other people, to concentrate on essentials.
And finally you're free, you're new, different from where you were,
and life itself starts to lead you, spreading out before you.
To love God and trust your own gifts. Even with the limitations.
The hard parts of the story.

There is a key event in Ignatius biography, you have probably heard,
how he went through a long recovery from a military wound

Selected Homilies

to be able to walk again. And as he spent the time, drifting in his mind,
then coming to read the Gospels and wonder about Jesus and his future,
he awakened to want a new life, not just more of the same in the royal court or the military field or pursuit of women,
but something along the lines of a dedicated life of service.
He stayed with this, went through the effort.
He came to understand himself, and maybe he could help other people
get through their own struggles, just as he was finding life.
To do this he had to set aside one way of life for another:
he took on a new role of a pilgrim, a hermit for awhile.
Even those changes came at first from his own Ego needs.
He says in his remembering these days,
waking up from his painful limitations, the healing,
God had to lead him from day to day like a school boy.

I'm glad Ignatius took notes, and learned to listen to the good spirits
inviting him to trust God in all the troubles, as a loved sinner, a new man.
And how in everything, as you come to love God, in gratitude,
all things work together for good, even from the beginning.

I see this in people, how the important wisdom
is not to figure out how to solve your problems, but instead
to take your whole story, that whole mess as it is,
directly putting it before God, like Ignatius laying down his armor.
You learn what happened and what you hope for, and then
you let it go, sell it all, give it to God:
your wounds and regrets and worries. Let go of it. Give it over.
Selling what you have, is coming to trust a new source of life,
even the hard parts, as the slogan goes: "let go, let God."

This is saying yes to our limits and vulnerability, all we carry,
with the assurance that God is not waiting for you to solve things,
but God lives and joins you in all of it. Love loving you.
At that point, the field is yours, you have the treasure.

Richard Bollman, SJ

finding your church

26th Sunday, 1978
On the Sunday following the death of Pope John Paul I
University of San Francisco

If there is any encouragement in Christ, any solace in love,
any participation in the Spirit, any compassion and mercy,
complete my joy by being of the same mind,
with the same love, united in heart, thinking one thing.
Do nothing out of selfishness or out of vainglory;
rather, humbly regard others as more important than yourselves,
each looking out not for his own interests,
but [also] everyone for those of others.
Have among yourselves the same attitude that is also yours in Christ Jesus.
(Philippians 2:1-5)

HOMILY

In the week ahead, our imaginations will probably spend a good bit of the time
in Rome, while the Cardinals come together to elect a Pope.
But this morning, I'd prefer to call up for you a part of the world
a few hundred miles farther east of Italy, where the Mediterranean
reaches wide and serenely up between the coasts of Greece and Turkey.
This is the Aegean Sea.
Perhaps you've travelled there, or remember it from geography books.
It is a maze of islands and peninsulas,
sun-drenched and incredibly deep indigo in color.
Dark as a good wine, Homer said of it in his poetry.
This is the sea Agamemnon sailed to Troy, about 150 miles across.
And the apostle Paul crossed it at least twice in his missionary work.

Selected Homilies

Picture him in a small boat
setting out with a few companions from a port very near ancient Troy,
navigating northwest across the upper corner of the Aegean
by way of the Island of Samothrace,
toward the northernmost territory of Greece.
There Paul lands for the first time in Europe, at a town called Neapolis.
He is about forty.

He does not linger in the port city, but moves inland
fifty miles to the Roman colony of Philippi.
A river flows near the town, hardly more than a stream, rather like the Jordan,
and it was a favorite gathering place for Jews
who had migrated to this part of the world.
They came to the river to pray, there being no synogogue in Philippi.
Here at the river, Paul joins a group of Jews at their prayer,
and according to his custom, he speaks to them
directly and passionately of the Risen Jesus
who has transformed his own life,
his view of history, his religious traditions, his whole way of being.
A woman in the group named Lydia invites Paul to her home.
Out of that community by the river
Paul founds the first Christian Church in Europe.

The Church at Philippi seems to have been
Paul's most successful missionary achievement.
Six years later, from prison probably in Ephesus,
Paul writes to this church a letter full of love and personal regard,
without a single hint of criticism or desire to correct anyone. Rare for Paul.
He seems to write out of personal need to stay in touch,
to celebrate his friendship with this community.
"I thank my God whenever I think of you," he says,
"and every time I pray for you I am happy. . . .
You have a permanent place in my heart.
God knows how much I miss you all."
And later in the letter Paul tells them
he is sending back to Philippi a young man from the Church there
who had been helping Paul on his journeys preaching.

Richard Bollman, SJ

And Epaphroditus, as he was called, was eager to return.
He had been ill--his old friends at Philippi had heard of it,
and though he was well now, he thought it best
to return home personally to reassure his family.
And Paul agreed.
The letter is full of personal remarks and details like these.
Epaphroditus may have delivered it.

Part of the letter was read here to us this morning.
The apostle's heart seems so open in these phrases,
giving encouragement and needing encouragement too,
reminding the Philippians simply of what faith can do among them.
"In the name of the encouragement you owe me in Christ,
in the name of the peace and reassurance that your love can bring me,
in the name of our fellowship, of tenderness, of compassion--
I beg you," he says, "live together faithfully,
at one in your convictions in your hearts and souls.
You have nothing to fear from each other,"
in other words; no reason to compete. You are not rivals,
but sisters, brothers, believers together.
Let Christ's own heart and mind be in you.

Here is the apostle writing to the Church,
telling them to really be the Church, without hesitation,
that in their fellowship and service to one another,
the death and resurrection of Jesus still takes place.
The dynamism of their community need never end.

The Church today is so very much larger and more far-flung
than the dozen or so Christian groups Paul knew before his death.
The tone of communication from Rome, or even from a local chancery,
rarely sounds as pertinent and personally addressed
as Paul's words to the community he touched at the riverbank,
whose names he knew and called out to from prison:
Lydia, Evodia, Epaphroditus, Clement, people whose homes he stayed at.
It is true, there are occasions
when we can feel at one with millions, like these months

Selected Homilies

when we have been able to mourn together for a Pope's death,
and then witness the coronation of John Paul,
whose goodness and disarming smile reached out to touch us
almost as immediately as Paul's letter would have touched
his friends at Philippi.
We hope to be so blessed again,
with a Pope of genuine warmth, faith, humanity.

But whoever he is,
once he is elected and the ceremonies are finished,
and the TV set cools, and the covers of TIME begin to stack up with other news,
once that happens, our felt sense of identity with millions
will be less easy to call up for consolation.
In this large Church of the World it is easy
to feel small, lost, or indifferent.

That is why, especially now, when our thoughts turn to Rome,
I want to remind you of that small community, that Church at Philippi,
that group of friends who--amazingly enough--
did not have to live as rivals with each other, or fearful,
but who consoled one another in sickness
and who coaxed from each other the best values
and the joy of being alive.
Where is that Church now?

It is here, wherever this letter is read and cherished.
It exists for you in whatever homes hold for you
the presence of Christ and the courage to believe.
What shall happen in Rome is important, yes,
and the Spirit of God moves and breathes there;
but remember too that the Spirit lives in the small Church as well,
the local gathering on the riverbank,
or in the college residence hall, or the hospital sickroom.
Or the family table in your homes.
Yes, Christ shall be present on earth in the future Pope,
but what difference can that make for me
if I do not also know Christ's presence in a
community of believers who I can see and talk to,

Richard Bollman, SJ

if I do not also find him in people who open my heart and life,
and who make testimony to me of their own daily death and rising.

According to Jesus,
at the center of God's kingdom, at its very heart,
there is no baroque cathedral, no severe formalities,
no hierarchies or religious professionals.
There is instead a gathering of friends in the Lord,
tax-collectors and prostitutes included.
Every rigor of living, every disappointment and ordinary evil,
every sin and sickness they have endured,
has emptied their spirits of illusion,
has stripped from their minds all self-concern and every easy belief.

It is Christ alone who fills them,
this community of friends,
with that hard and bright reality,
true faith, that diamond center,
and it is he who actually is alive in them
with a love that does not cling to itself,
but which moves and flows and gives.
May Christ so empty us, and live in us.

the comfort of time

4th Sunday, A
Matthew 5:1-12

"Blessed are the poor in spirit,
for theirs is the kingdom of heaven.
Blessed are they who mourn,

Selected Homilies

for they will be comforted.
Blessed are the meek,
for they will inherit the land." (Matthew 5:3-5)

HOMILY

I had a dream two nights ago that released a flood of memories
surrounding a death in my family, events long ago, but once again vivid.
I bring this up because memory drew me into this teaching of Jesus,
this telling of the great beatitudes, the happiness statements.

The beatitudes are not commandments.
Rather, they address the issue of happiness, grief or joy,
in the actual condition of our human life, what to expect, what to trust.
It's as if the ordinary limits of life connect us to a power,
the Kingdom of God, or the presence of God,
We go there through poverty, and mourning,
simplicity, mortality, and hope.

And this came clearer to me in my memories, as I said, of a death.
The person who died was a two year old child, a boy, my nephew,
and my sister's second born. Mikie, we called him.
Fifty some years ago it was; and it was so simple and heart breaking.
The boy was at play in the driveway of the neighbors house,
down low, making little noise,
and the car as it gently exited the drive simply struck him once on the head,
and that was it. No one saw it directly, though his three year old brother
was at play nearby. It all came as a stunning accident, and it cut through
the whole family, a brutal crash of loss, grief, this ache.
Like I say, a long time back, my sister too is now deceased,
but there it comes up again so important in a dream.

Not many other details are known to me: I was in the seminary,
so I could only visualize the gathering of the family, the coroner's report.

Richard Bollman, SJ

The funeral. Old seminary rules applied, I could not travel home.
I have no interior knowledge of how it felt for my sister and her husband.
Except, of course, I do know—there is a common grief
that spreads through the family, that stays there,
that awakens me from a dream 50 years later.

And there's this I can report, from my sister's letters.
This is what takes me to the beatitudes.
The story appeared in the local papers, and she told me
they began to receive notes from strangers, from anyone who had
a similar grief, a story to tell, that same anguish
which found its way into little cards and letters sent to their house.

She said, no one was giving advice or telling us to feel better.
It was just a help, not to be alone in the heart of this,
not to be alone there. And she quoted to me what one person said,
"Your only friend now is Time." She quoted that.
I believe that in a kind of friendship with Time
she found some breathing space.

Here's what I see, looking back, from my adult perspective.
The letters from strangers, and the mere passing of time itself,
maybe an hour or a day, maybe a week, this goes by
and it was all something you could only receive. You could let it happen,
and let it be. Receive it and let it go.
And in that allowing, receiving, a breathing space opens up.
There comes a connection to something other than your own self,
your own loss, something besides that, which you receive;
which begins to exist and show itself.
And that is what Jesus called comfort. The comfort of a presence,
of God, of the Kingdom, of grace. That beatitude.

As a spiritual writer Cynthia Bourgeault says, "if we can remain open,
we discover that a mysterious 'something' does indeed reach back
to comfort us; the tendrils of our grief trailing out into the unknown
become intertwined with a greater love that holds all things together."

Selected Homilies

Last spring I heard a good teacher say,
"When God finds an empty space in us, God will fill it."
And I noticed how my tendency, when I feel empty,
is to fill that empty space myself, with all kinds of solutions.
Like blaming, eating and drinking, spreading complaints.
But instead, the emptiness and frustration is a doorway
to poverty of spirit, a leaning in toward purity of heart,
starting to be the peace you want to have.

This is a summation, then, of the beatitudes.
"When God finds an empty space, God will fill it."
Unexpected gifts can come. Blessedness. The kingdom.
Time is on our side.

The spiritual writer quoted above is Cynthia Bourgeault from *The Wisdom Jesus*, © 2008, p. 43. Reprinted by arrangement with Shambhala Publications, Inc., Boulder, CO. www.shambhala.com.

through the narrow door

21st Sunday, C

He passed through towns and villages, teaching as he went and making his way to Jerusalem. Someone asked him, "Lord, will only a few people be saved?" He answered them, "Strive to enter through the narrow door, for many, I tell you, will attempt to enter but will not be strong enough." (Luke 13:22-24)

Richard Bollman, SJ

HOMILY

Yesterday around lunch time,
as I was looking through some of this scripture
in the study on the first floor of our Jesuit community,
the doorbell rang. I wasn't sure anybody else was at home,
so I put my book down and walked to the front hallway,
four steps above the front door,
where outside a young man was looking in, waiting.
He had this eager restlessness about him, almost pacing,
but happy and expectant.
It was as if he had erased any of that falseness or formality
we can sometimes wear as we knock on a door:
his readiness was transparent.
And then right away I met Jim Hoff who had come to the door
from the other side of the house.
So I said "Hi" to Jim, and "I guess you're expecting this young guy,"
and he said yes, he was, it was his nephew, his sister's boy,
and the third of them to come to Xavier as a freshman.

So I had a sense why the young man was out there, perfectly focused
on being welcomed and met by his uncle.
I said, "well, I'm glad to see you back" to Jim,
just a casual remark, an exit line,
since he had been away for a number of weeks,
and then I moved away back to my study
not wanting to intrude on the personal moment there at the door.

But I've thought back on it. How good to be welcomed like that,
to ring the doorbell, and pace around and look through the glass,
and be expected and received by the brother of your mother.
A great way to come to a new place, this first year at college,
this embrace, this "Wow, I know you, I love you, and you're here at last."

Selected Homilies

I picture myself standing at the door of life itself.
That precious opening, but we'll be there one day, right?
Even today, you might be there, at this narrow place, where life is at stake.
I picture myself looking through the window,
knocking, ringing the doorbell, but wondering.
Hoping. Pointing to myself. Hey it's me, right? Are we ready?
(You know what I mean?)
And I listen, and I wait, for The Householder . . . what will happen,
what will be that greeting.

At such a place, you want to be known, in touch, in blood relationship
with the owner of the house, the source of life itself.
You can't just be a casual bystander . . . .
"Well, I've belonged to a fairly decent culture, a good parish,
I've had the best education, and I know all about you:
you remember, I taught all about you at our schools,
I've eaten and drunk at your table!"

What could be missing? Here, at the door of life.
ME, I could be missing.
It isn't who you know, it's what you've done, of course, and who you actually are.
To be a true Israelite, that's what's called for.
Loving my people, my neighbors, with my heart and strength,
avoiding the traps of greed and competition,
paying attention to the homeless, the child at risk, the refugee . . . .
Yes, this would make me more secure at the door of life.
But what Jesus suggests is even more mysterious, more challenging.

We enter the narrow gate, he says, through our STRIVING.
Through our agony. That's what the word means.
To strive . . . in the Greek of Luke, it is the word for the essential struggle of life,
the AGON, the battleground, that is unique and personal for each of us.
STRIVE with your life, live it in its essential struggle.
This is the word that describes all the great dramatic conflicts:
the Agon is what makes Antigone to be Antigone, Hamlet to be Hamlet.
Even the failure in the midst of gift, the sinfulness despite all the blessing;
everything about you that perhaps you want to change. Don't grind your teeth,

Richard Bollman, SJ

enter through it, trusting the life that you are given.
There you find the blood kinship with God,
in the blood you shed just to be yourself:
fearlessly taking on the body and soul you have, the kinships,
the social and civil era. One's AGON, one's agony,
that which makes Mother Teresa to be Mother Teresa,
or Karen to be Karen, David to be David,
me to be myself, and in this gaunt recognition
to find God my brother, my mother, my father.
At the creative root of life.

This is what saves us, this engagement with where we find ourselves,
neither grandiose nor running away and hiding.
Will there be many or few who come through? Who knows?
"Strive to enter by the narrow gate."

Here is a story, one of many around us, about that narrow place.
Bob Beckman, a Jesuit now in his seventies, went to work in Peru
more than twenty years ago. Some of you know him.
He returns to his native Cincinnati every few summers,
more frequently now as family members are aging, and
then he goes back, as always, to the different world of his adopted homeland.
He wrote once, how he felt that return, that re-entry.
"After the flight and a welcome in Lima," he said,
"I had to board the slow and uncertain public bus for Arequipa.
It was a long drive south, along the seacoast.
The bus left late, as it always does. I had a wooden seat at the window,
thirsting for fresh air, and then a very large woman
sat next to me with two little children, and a chicken.
I scrunched up, remembering the ease of a private car in the States,
feeling my life narrow down to this overheated and very smelly bus trip.
And tightened in my seat, looking out the window I watched
the sun go down into the ocean,
the moon rise over the mountains;
and the children next to me, after some hours, asleep with their mother
watching them in such a look of love.
And I took in a deep breath, without any criticism or defense.
I crossed over. I was home."

Selected Homilies

He slipped through the narrow door. That's what it's like.
Our iniquity falls away into the sheer purgation of the struggle.
A blood relationship, our own kin, claims us.
We are ourselves. Even the least of us, are then and there first.
And only we can do this striving, ours to wrestle with.
Amen, for the truth of it, the gift of it.

2. THE ADVENT OF GOD

There are many kinds of new years: Chinese, Jewish, Aztec; personal birth-days, academic new years, and this, the Christian New Year, the season of Advent. It resounds with the voice of John the Baptist, Isaiah, Jesus, calling us not to assess our losses or make resolutions, but to awaken to our desire for something more. It speaks of God's coming, the certainty of it, just for the sake of being with us, sinners as we are.

wakeful time

1st Sunday of Advent, A

"...you know the time;
it is the hour now for you to awake from sleep.
For our salvation is nearer now than when we first believed;
the night is advanced, the day is at hand." (Romans 13:11-12a)

HOMILY

So what is this Advent "waking?"
Put it this way.
It's like, in the middle of the night, or just past the middle,
it simply happens, you wake up, not with a jolt,

but getting a feel for something, some quality of your own life.
Tired, but not tired.
Your hearing is sharp, differentiated in the dark.
Moreover you actually notice, notice what you hear.
This is "listening."

There is no urgency in this moment, but just a prompting,
and a simplicity now to simply stay awake.
Eyes grow accustomed to the dark, to objects in the room,
some noticing even of color, the dark shades and a glint of light here or there.

Stay with this moment now.
You feel the presence of yourself.
And a larger presence, a sensing. Of course. Who are you with?
Sense the warmth, the hum of sleep, a spouse nearby,
or the other sleepers in the house. Even your neighbor's house:
an inner sensing, a satisfaction, or a wrenching: your heart goes out.

But then pull your heart back to your own body.
Allow your bodily movement to carry you, up and out of bed.
The first kinks and stretches and deeper breaths, this easy shift.
"It is time now to wake from sleep."
Day is not here yet; but it is close.
You can sense it. Night is far gone.
But it is not Christmas: not the dawn of a special event,
but simply an inner prompting from your own nervous system,
your muscles and heart, to awaken.

You stand, you go where you like, to the window, the waning stars,
to a big chair maybe in the living room,
just to sit awhile, under a woolen throw, still awake: very few thoughts.
Spongy mind. Alert ears. Alert eyes.
You see without turning on the lights, now more and more,
hearing the tick of appliances, a passing car,
letting your feet remember the textures and distances
that guided you to the chair.

Richard Bollman, SJ

This is watching, this is keeping vigil,
this is "not knowing" the day or the hour.
What is supposed to happen? Maybe nothing.
This is the prayer of adult life,
sitting with soft mind and alert senses,
letting the circumstances of your life emerge to speak as they wish
in the living room: a family photo, a newspaper from last night,
a cup of cold coffee,
and the routine impulse to clean it up, to complete a task,
but you let is pass, it subsides, no need to set out yet.
But feel what it is to remember the unwritten letter,
to care for a home, to catch yesterday's headline of maybe
a break in the Somalia blockade, maybe an upsurge in retail spending.
Listen, feel, see, taste all this.
The forgiven. The unforgiven.

And in the quiet: a Presence. Did someone come in?
Or is someone simply and already here with me.
"Our salvation is nearer now
than when we first believed."
Indeed, is it you? Nearer than when I first believed,
nearer than when I had a lot to say, my prayers to you;
nearer than when I knew your name, knew all about you,
knew what you wanted.
My knowing is very slim now.
But you are nearer than when I first believed,
nearer in the dark before the daylight comes.

How good it is to spend wakeful time, watchful time,
without judging it or wrenching it one way or another!

I remember just a few days back, the day after Thanksgiving,
setting out for a movie,
and simply becoming slowly aware that I didn't want to see anything of the kind,
but I stopped in a park on the way,

Selected Homilies

remembering the family dinner the afternoon before, familiar arguments,
letting it come back in a long, listening glance now.
No regrets, no apology, open to feel myself, ourselves,
an ache for something to be made really new.

What do you wait for?
feel it, let the desire for a new heart
take over.

winter welcome

1st Sunday of Advent, C
1 Thessalonians 3:12 - 4:2; Luke 21:25-36

There will be signs in the sun, the moon, and the stars, and on earth nations will be in dismay, perplexed by the roaring of the sea and the waves. But when these signs begin to happen, stand erect and raise your heads because your redemption is at hand. (Luke 21:25)

. . . may the Lord make you increase and abound in love for one another and for all, just as we have for you . . . (1 Thessalonians 3:12)

HOMILY

I'd like to enter the season of Advent here from a personal point of view.
December begins my last month being pastor at Bellarmine,
so I am at the point of expecting something new for myself,

Richard Bollman, SJ

something new of God, not sure what that shall be.
I do have some clarity: there are these four weeks in December,
and then I'll have some days in January to pack up,
and then January 13 I fly west to a sabbatical program in what they call
"applied" theology for people in pastoral work: not all of them Catholic,
not all of them from the States.
So that's out there, in expectation. The known facts.
But that's not the core of Advent for me, what I am drawn to.

I keep wanting to feel the preciousness of the time that is Now.
To sink into it with care and trust. Time and place right now: so valuable.
I think this is the bottom rung of the Advent season, that savoring.
In times of the roaring seas and nature shaken to its core,
in times even of apprehension and uncertainty,
don't drift off into the blunted feelings of our addictive culture,
don't drift off into the daily anxious rush.
Be vigilant, raise your head. Right now. That's the word.
It's what I long for. Something of life very close.

I have a custom on weekends when I can manage it,
to take the scripture and a note pad to a restaurant,
maybe breakfast at First Watch, or mid-morning coffee at Starbucks.
Yesterday it was the Joseph Beth café, which in the dying light of afternoon
seemed like an old English pub. I sat at a table on the raised platform,
the carpeted area up the two steps, at the side wall of shelving
and an open ledge where they've placed a Christmas tree,
a few feet high, lit and decorated, so I had a good view of
all the room in pools of light, dark wood, mostly empty tables.
I ordered a Winter Welcome Ale, their cheapest bottle, new to the menu,
really perfect to deepen my involvement in the moment, the precious time.
As it turns out Winter Welcome is an English ale from Yorkshire.
The bottle has this to say: "this seasonal beer. . . . limited edition,
(I copied this down),
is brewed for the short days and long nights of winter.
And should be contemplated before an open fire."

Selected Homilies

Even without the the fire, I found a contemplative solitude opening up.
A sense of place, taking in the familiar. The chairs and tables around me
each had their ghosts of previous visits, that corner spot, that booth,
with friends who filled the moment. Now, this precious time is the present.
Everything in place, all of life becoming full.
In the quiet, a deep love and stability held me, well beyond the beer.
Memory and gratitude, the late afternoon light, all of it a grace.
The season of Advent, the great waiting, a spirit of expectation,
how it seems to arrive in the gift of solitude, through our senses alert.
There it is, not far. You can sense it even now;
or on your own back deck some morning, or by a fire pit, or gratefully
with your family where the TV is turned off,
and maybe a card game begins. Miracles of presence.
Be vigilant, raise your head. It is so near.

A mother and two children arrived before long,
the little girl maybe seven years old, the boy about four;
the girl exceptionally tuned to the occasion, a supper in a café this evening,
poised at the table right at the edge of the platform where I sat.
The boy kept pulling his mom toward those short steps,
wanting a platform table too, and she said,
"No Henry, right down here." He lingered, touched the railings,
moved then behind his mother's table, a big booth, running his hands
across the booth table, the upholstered bench. "No, right here, Henry."
Opposite his sister.

Mother was soon served a red wine,
and the children something with straws, and they inspected the menu.
She said to the server: "soon my husband will come, and our baby."
And they brought a high chair, and after I poured the rest
of Winter Welcome Ale and started writing,
her husband arrived, and the baby, who claimed the devoted attention
of the older children. Henry kept moving from his place
to each corner of the table, agog with so much to feel and wonder about.

Paul said to his early friends at Thessalonika,
"the Lord will make you strong by your love for one another.

Conduct yourselves by that affection, blameless in holiness."
The richness of the time overflowed around me, the solitude
and now the hospitality of the family together cherishing its moment.
The season of the Lord's coming: it unfolds without asking,
when we give it a moment of attention, vigilance,
the solitude of a place you love, the attention of a friend or a child,
open space, friendly space, and all at once a vital space
of the divine presence underlying everything.
As if in our waiting, God is tangible already,
and finally we have a chance to notice it happily and courageously,
an answer to our fear, a silencing of the roaring seas.
A mother arranging us at the table.

Think of those early communities of Christ believers,
Thessalonika, Corinth, Rome: who were those men and women,
workers, artisans, weavers, slaves, sailors,
pagans all, who were ready to give up wasting their affection
in the old addictive cults of nature gods,
and the helplessness of a socially rigid caste system.
They had found something altogether more alive and promising.
there was the story of a forgiving God, tangibly present in the community,
inspiring service and just ways. The Christ has come. The best of us.

Who are we coming to be, together here? Something wonderful
that I hope will never stop being attractive and essential to your lives.
This season allows us to savor it: the love that lies deep underneath
a conflicted and addictive society, bringing the anxiety to stillness.

It comes alive as you savor the time, the time you have when you stop.
As you notice the place, with all your senses, as if for the first time.
Be vigilant. Raise you head.

Selected Homilies

the wilderness road

2nd Sunday of Advent, B
Isaiah 40:1-11, 2 Peter 3:8-14, Mark 1:1-8

This morning's words from Isaiah are a kind of poem about homecoming. Going home now to rebuild, everyone together. All of it happening through the power of God, and according to God's timing. The events spoken of occurred in the middle 6th century BC, the return of the people from their exile in Babylon and the rebuilding of Judaism in Israel. The familiarity of the promise should not allow us to forget the hard work of trust, and walking the way that opens up. We who trust God are always standing on the brink of something new. And we stand in the promise, not the fulfillment.

HOMILY

So these people crossing the wilderness,
seem sheltered in a great gesture of comfort from the Lord's heart.
But what do we understand of this effort on the ground,
how can we get close to it?
It happened in the middle of the 6th century, B.C.
A generation of Jews, many hundreds surely,
have been encouraged to leave Babylon,
packing up and going on foot, back to their own country.
We can check the facts this way:
it happened through a shift in politics nobody expected:
the despotic power of Babylon was thrown out by Cyrus of Persia
and he wanted to release all the exiles in that country
to let them return home to where they belonged.
But to get close to the experience, to feel our way into it,
look at this situation: many of the people returning were under 40!
They had been born in Babylon,
and had never even seen Israel, or the great citadel of Jerusalem.
It was all stories till now.

Richard Bollman, SJ

Imagine the inner experience for them, the chance for a new start
where they really belonged now. And yet the work of it ahead.
Taking on the valleys and hills, counting on God's blessing,
what shall it be for them.

Bring it closer. Coming home: it's what many thousands of people want
in the American south, people who had lived through
hurricane Katrina, in New Orleans.
To leave the hotel rooms and shelters and to start over
on the ground where they belong.
We haven't met them, but we see their pictures,
and we can identify, more with the immediacy of it,
a world we know, and sharing a longing like that;
We know about home town, and neighborhood, and belonging.

All the more, the whole country asks right now every day;
how to bring the military troops back from Iraq.
Can you imagine that desire, for safety again
and for a future you can count on.
"Your warfare is accomplished, says your God,
you have gone through double what you deserve."

Homecoming, release, good news, a future.
We who live secure lives, we feel it too.
We wait for a biopsy, we set out on recovery from an illness,
we hope for a reconciliation in a family, or a job.
But it's so often a long long time we wait.
With God, the scripture says, one year is as a thousand.
Our timing is not the only timing.

There's this great wilderness in front of us then,
where a political shift has released people as the prophet sings of it,
a story of struggle, and the long journey,
where you can only let yourself start to hope.
Open yourself to this, to be touched. I feel we're all caught up in it.
You can't help but know about these far-flung longings.

Selected Homilies

My own attention to Iraq was caught up again this weekend.
You may have read of the bomb that killed ten marines on Friday in Falluja,
and wounded eleven more: you read and try to figure out,
how did this happen: a land mine, a suicide, the details are vague.
Then on page ten, a picture of three marines in stunned grief,
not in Falluja but in Camp Pendleton, dealing with this news.
And these young men are not vague at all, but flesh and blood;
not in military uniform but t-shirts and fatigues.
They stand at the edge of a sidewalk, facing off into the distance,
not looking at each other, each with their thoughts and sorrow.
How young they are and vulnerable, and here it is,
a soldier's worst fear, these improvised explosive devices,
happening even to a foot patrol. No vehicle, no armor.

You feel with these young men, looking at the picture,
and I begin to think we have to let our feelings teach us
that truth which is more accurate,
deeper than we can get from any political or military analysis.
There it is: as long as marines are killed every few days, a few or a dozen,
and as they are stopped in their tracks,
so are you stopped in your morning as you read.
When any nation is at war we also struggle with it at home,
as the military fight it out far away:
whether they are your friends or sons out there,
or just people you read about.
Maybe it's the uncounted number of Iraqi civilians,
but even so we're in this together, I think.
It is our shared story with all the homeless.

It doesn't matter your political party.
It is a waiting time and a wilderness time, for a long time,
and in such a season we all feel displaced and fearful.
Like we all feel scarred by the hurricanes, the homelessness.
Like in the Church, we all feel abused or discredited,
when any one person is abused or put down or disqualified.
And so this is a season about our wilderness walk,

Richard Bollman, SJ

this is Advent. And we walk with a crowd.
Hope is just beyond the horizon, but not yet in sight.

It is a time, then, for great tenderness,
tenderness in all things,
toward ourselves, and toward everybody who is ill at ease
or wandering from home.
We can start this tenderness right away:
just by letting ourselves feel what is the matter now,
feel what is at stake, even across the aisle from you.
Appreciating what is happening to people,
this is the tenderness of God.
Comfort my people, comfort them.

We know that long road, that storm-shattered street, withered field,
and look across to where there may be something of the promise
not yet glimpsed, to bring us through. A hopeful time,
though the hope is without any certainty, without even any specifics.
It's a rough place: who will make it smooth?

Let your feelings and affections, your fear and your tenderness for life,
help you to know the heart of this time. This Advent.
Let the scripture come to you in your fingertips, your taste and love for life.
Don't be afraid of the confusion and the connections with other people
that your senses will involve you in! Morning after morning.
This is a kind of intimacy that helps to bond us as human beings.

Peter's letter suggests that when we get close to the longing in this way
we hasten the coming of the day of God.
Surely it does more good to be close to our shared suffering
rather than to argue it down or deny it or blame it on someone.

We come to the river Jordan here,
or to the Mississippi, or the Ohio, our toes in the mud,
with the other sinners of our town:

Selected Homilies

because here is the beginning of the Good News.
And only the beginning
And maybe a new beginning, like never having heard it before.
Day by day, our longing hastens something new to happen.
We find a home in that possibility.

the river of repentance

2nd Sunday of Advent, B
Mark 1:1-5

As it is written in Isaiah the prophet:
"Behold, I am sending my messenger ahead of you;
he will prepare your way.
A voice of one crying out in the desert:
'Prepare the way of the Lord,
make straight his paths.'"
John [the] Baptist appeared in the desert
proclaiming a baptism of repentance for the forgiveness of sins.
People of the whole Judean countryside and all the inhabitants of Jerusalem were going out to him and were being baptized by him in the Jordan River as they acknowledged their sins. (Mark 1:2-5)

HOMILY

So John calls to us from the Jordan River;
and the season, the word itself, calls out for us to go.
Go to the Jordan, where many people begin to go now,
coming to yield to change, to a new time,

Richard Bollman, SJ

to let John baptize them, repenting of their sins,
this baptism of forgiveness.

There is a photograph of me at the Jordan River with my father.
It was taken on a tour there, a pilgrimage, in 1976.
He was 81, I was 38.
We stand looking at the camera from a stairway
that goes down to the water behind us.
There are a few boats in the distance.
Our arms are around each other.
My dad carries a cane.
We look directly at the camera.
It is quite a moment.

This was a journey of atonement, I think we both knew.
Mother was dead now about a year. It was our time.
It's what we would do, though we didn't do it often together:
that is, we were risk takers, and could set out for a new place.
I had to deal with my fears, for sure. I'm not sure what he might have dealt with.
His face, as often in photos, is serene and proud, and a bit unrevealing.
As for me, I have brown hair, I squint in the strong light,
I look 28, wanting to appear confident, but mainly managing.

There we are at the river: the river of Time, river of Change,
river of the forgiveness of sins.

We had taken earlier trips together, where our misalliance was painful:
his desire to show me a football game at Notre Dame
is one I most especially remember with embarrassment at my resistance.
I think the Holy Land pilgrimage helped heal those breaches.
It is such slow work.

After his death, ten years later, I found a card I had sent him for Father's Day,
only months before my mother died: his wife and friend through so much.
"I'll call if I can" the card said.

Selected Homilies

That summer of change for him, losing her.
My journey to a workshop, the card sent off.
I believe I did not call. He kept the card.
I look back now with compassion upon us both
who we were at the Jordan.
The slow work of healing goes on.

Advent again this year.
It is not the repeat of a season,
not starting over either,
but getting a vantage point.
Go to the river, your own river of changes, or time.
Think back to your last visit there, a year ago, five years.
Who you were then?
Maybe it's time to leaf through old photo albums.
You see in your face, back then, back through the changes,
some glimpses of your desire to be human, to be free.
To love well, maybe.
How slow it goes: is anything happening?

And through this river of our own humanity there comes One
Mightier than we are, in the flesh with us,
who baptizes with the Holy Spirit and with fire,
for the gradual healing of wounds, the integration of relationships,
the education of the heart.
It happens, beyond our doing.

We know it through our own desiring.
Slowly coming up out of the water.

Richard Bollman, SJ

the reed not shaken

3rd Sunday of Advent, A

When John heard in prison of the works of the Messiah,
he sent his disciples to him with this question,
"Are you the one who is to come, or should we look for another?"
Jesus said to them in reply, "Go and tell John what you hear and see:
the blind regain their sight, the lame walk,
lepers are cleansed, the deaf hear, the dead are raised,
and the poor have the good news proclaimed to them." (Matthew 11:2-5)

HOMILY

Jesus had to sort out his options, his way of faith.
Here he is a young Jew, in a time of some national difficulties
and a time of religious factions,
but what is his faith to be like, what religious practice?
How will he live a responsible life.

The chief national difficulty was Roman occupation.
Roman rule was not unusual in all parts of the Mediterranean
but their practice was to just accept tribute, keep peace,
and let the local rulers run the county.
That had worked under Herod the Great.
Even though the situation was a religious violation,
Herod was shrewd at accommodation.
But he died when Jesus was a child.
After him, the kingdom of Israel was divided among three heirs,
and the current Herod, called Antipas,
was not able to keep down the rebellious religious Zealots.
Rome had to intervene to quell rebellion: many Zealots were crucified.

Selected Homilies

Pontius Pilate became the local authority in Judea when Jesus was 12.
The Zealot party was still alive, underground,
and even one of his own followers was called Simon the Zealot.
But Jesus did not follow their agenda, though they wished him to:
"when will you restore the kingdom," they often asked.

No, Jesus would not sponsor violent intervention to restore Israel.
But there were religious solutions proposed: the reform of the spirit of Israel.
The Pharisees, for example, were a devout sect,
known for their renewed interest in the scripture and ritual Law,
how it gave a distinct direction to life different from the pagans.
The Sadducees were another Jewish sect, more conservative,
not wanting to tamper with the old ways,
and not wanting to call attention to any ideological conflict with Rome.
They liked stability, in thought, behavior, politics.
But though Jesus enjoyed dialogue, even debate with these movements,
there is no record of any adherence with them.
They didn't persuade Jesus or guide his priorities.

What shaped Jesus' religious and social imagination
was the preaching and religious practice of John in the wilderness.
John he sought out. He was baptized.
And that especially was a spiritual experience for Jesus.

Jesus, then, was helped by John's view of the crisis of the era:
that God's intervention was very close upon the nation,
and so it was important to be alert, but very patient.
It was important to live an ethical life, but not to blame or take sides
against people. Everybody could come to the river.
It was important not to put your trust just in group identity,
being a Pharisee or Sadducee, a Jew or Roman, even:
the main thing is to be awake, and to do the next right thing.

If I could sum it up, in critical times there is a tendency
to manage things by reform movements, or by violence.
These efforts often lead to factions and self-righteousness,

Richard Bollman, SJ

or to bloodshed.
And they overlook the fact that what we're dealing with
is a spiritual illness, a falling back from trust in God,
and the unleashing of some addictive tendencies:
greed, taking care of number one, resentments, vengeance.

What's needed instead is a certain kind of faith:
which I would call "readiness to receive what we can't achieve on our own."
Whether your goal is to live in better health or sobriety,
or to find courage to work for justice,
or to reconcile the tensions and resentments that have grown up
in some of your relationships,
you have to begin from the point of view
that God's power is what is required, and it is already close to you.

That was a spirituality Jesus himself took on,
and he let it inform his own choices and preaching.
This kernel of it came from the ministry of John,
that, and from the people at the river, that messy and mixed group.
They shared a common passion: to find hope, and a sense of belonging.

In them, I like to think, Jesus found allies,
in the poor and the marginal.
Because for them, the promises of God were important:
the fearful, the disabled, the ones not able to live the holiness laws.
They revealed to Jesus the circumstances where God would intervene:
God wouldn't be collaborating with our own plans for renewal;
God wouldn't be collaborating with a rebellion against Rome.
But God would be very much able to enter our circumstances
among people who had a vulnerable, open readiness for change.
They were ready to receive what they couldn't achieve on their own.

What would that feel like to be in John's frame of mind,
not a reed shaken by the wind,
thrown off by every religious controversy or trend.
Not a lover of compromise nor just a consumer of the right religion,

Selected Homilies

looking for the most elite or progressive parish.
No, John was one who could stand in this wilderness of temptation
and be himself, unshaken, a prophet tuned in to the grace of God.

What is it like to turn with John's mind to our own times,
these very conditions around us, of broken promises and civil wars,
of uncertain job stability, lost mortgages, and a disillusioned church–
all this is nothing we can fix with self-righteousness, blame, or violence.
Rather we trust the Advent of God, in Jesus
who does not desert us, never stands far off from the ache of our needs.
He shall announce a new hope for justice after every failure.
This hope will arise from solidarity together as a community,
a gifted and blessed body.
And in awakening faith of this kind, as Jesus did,
the demons left, the paralysis loosened.

Take it on for yourself.
Advent moves along too quickly, and of course
we're often running around, being consumers,
or fussing and gossiping and blaming the world as always.
But then there's the mind of John the Baptist:
it invites us to consider a place in ourselves
where we do not need to be afraid.
But instead we're invited to be ready to receive
what we can't force to happen.
It is a deep place, this receptivity, deep as our breath,
and you can always find it, because we always breathe.
Think of it as a still place, where the reeds do not shake,
and where comfort or discomfort is not important,
but what grabs your attention is the rumor of Christ already here.

Richard Bollman, SJ

risking encounter

3rd Sunday of Advent, A

As they were going off,
Jesus began to speak to the crowds about John,
"What did you go out to the desert to see?
A reed swayed by the wind?
Then what did you go out to see?
Someone dressed in fine clothing?
Those who wear fine clothing are in royal palaces.
Then why did you go out? To see a prophet?
Yes, I tell you, and more than a prophet." (Matthew 11:7-9)

HOMILY

I was caught yesterday in some pre-Christmas grid-lock,
Saturday it was. I usually travel on Saturdays
with the scripture on my clip-board,
and I was on my way to a late breakfast, looking down occasionally,
looking down to the Gospel on the car seat next to me,
and looking out at the traffic.
Looking down, looking out.

"What did you go out to the desert to see?" says Jesus.

Among all these cars, all these people
at the intersection of Montgomery and Cooper Roads,
I'm probably the only one thinking about John the Baptist.
And the deserts of Judea seemed far away,
and a little bit attractive. I could use some space around me!

That's what John must have thought one day, somewhere in his mid-twenties.
John left the towns, left the traffic. "I need some space."
He went to the desert, like later monks did, men and women,
because they saw there has to be a better way,
because a lot of ordinary life seemed to miss the point.

This really happened—a movement of spirit among a small minority,
sometimes loners, sometimes in community,
trying to get closer to the truth of the Jewish way of life,
and later the Christian way of life,
off to the deserts around Jerusalem, Alexandria, Damascus,
looking for a way to really follow the path, the teaching, the Gospel,
to surrender to God, and to the Spirit of the light.

The desert is not sought out because it's restful, or close to nature.
When you're in the desert, you are quickly invited
to trust a lot more, to surrender.
Because the desert brings you close to danger, loneliness, dry times,
thieves in hiding,
but it's real, life is real there.
Some searchers found that God was close there.

So I look out of the car window and wonder.
Maybe nobody's thinking of John the Baptist,
but somebody surely is thinking, wanting, pondering,
"Isn't there a better way than this, something more wholesome,
something more of God, something closer to the truth?"
Questions, searching, goes on, every century, in the desert of the human heart.

That place! The heart!
Have any of you decided to go there?
To leave the grid-lock and find your heart.
That's the place of Advent. Your heart.
Of course, it's scary. That stony path, with its wild beasts,
its hungers, its dry times, its dangers.

Richard Bollman, SJ

Down there in the heart, even this night,
is there some secret desire for encounter with the Holy One,
a desire for a Savior God,
wanting to trust Jesus, not things, to follow the light.
Maybe something really big is happening to you,
something fearful, like illness, or confusing, like a broken friendship,
and there's no getting around the way your heart feels,
the kind of trust you want to live by now,
the kind of light you really need.
This is okay. Plunge in.

I met a woman who entered her heart, who faced her reality,
and found a body buried under the rubble,
and the body was herself. She needed to care again, to dig out.
I know a man who wanted to get into his heart,
but first he had to quit his job, and find a new way of working.
That is what happens when you want God for real,
not just ideas and dreams.

So you look out the window of your car,
and very likely, on the sidewalks, entering a shop, in the car next to you,
there are some desert people on the brink of entering their heart,
or wondering how to do that.
Maybe you are one of them.
Maybe you are John the Baptist, wondering about this Jesus you met,
or have heard about. "Are you the one who is to come?"

Gary Snyder is a poet I often enjoy,
an outdoorsman, a kind of desert person of the American northwest.
This former beatnik and wanderer has found direction in his writing.
One of his poems is about finding a poem:
how do they come to him? How is he guided?

He describes the poem coming as a forest animal
coming at night where he has camped and lit a fire,

Selected Homilies

but the poem itself is outside of the enclosure,
barely lit by the campfire, until it stirs.
And then it makes a noise among the boulders
and he goes to meet it.

This seems to me to be an Advent poem, a poem about
something that comes in the dark, surprisingly,
and we have to be careful, and attentive, and awake.
We could call this poem, "How my heart comes to me,"
(blundering over the boulders at night,
frightened outside the range of my campfire.)
We could call it "How Jesus comes to me,"
(outside the range of my campfire.
I go to meet him at the Edge of the light.)

Christmas is close now, don't you feel it, don't you sense the Coming!

the company of Mary

4th Sunday of Advent, B

Mary said to the angel,
"How can this be, since I have no relations with a man?"
And the angel said to her in reply, "The holy Spirit will come upon you,
and the power of the Most High will overshadow you.
Therefore the child to be born will be called holy, the Son of God."

Mary said, "Behold, I am the handmaid of the Lord." (Luke 1:34-35, 38)

Richard Bollman, SJ

HOMILY

So, if God makes a promise to a young woman that she will have a child,
think of it: very soon she can tell if the promise is real,
if it is being fulfilled. And a child is growing inside, and is born,
and yet even so everything that is to come is as yet undisclosed.
Like our own coming out of the womb:
for a while everything for our mother is focused and internal,
and then we're here and there's something unpredictable:
God's actual purpose in connecting a mother and child,
the purpose of a life is worked out in time, gradually.

It's important not to make Mary some kind of supernatural person.
The mother of Jesus becomes a believer in God's purpose all over again.
Not fully seeing where things shall lead.
Not much of what happened to Jesus looks like ascending the throne of David,
or reigning over the house of Jacob.
The angel was over enthusiastic, exaggerated.
Time will tell. Like us too, Mary is a searcher, a day at a time.
Luke describes her as one who frequently remembered events
held them in her heart, giving everything over, patient to understand things
when the time comes.
And it is that note of her existence that speaks of our Advent.

No matter how well we manage things and have them worked out,
we live our role in life, in Church, in family, in our culture,
we live it in hope for fulfillment. All is gift, all is hoped for.
It's a mystery unfolding: that's what we hear of Jesus story too,
of which we are a part. Something revealed only gradually,
and even yet not fully spoken.
Mystery: that's the word that described the sense of a purpose unfolding.

Sometime it seems to me that my real purpose in life
is something happening out of the corner of my eye,
not fully seen, a secret hidden even from myself.

Selected Homilies

That's the place, perhaps, just out of sight,
where Christ's story and ours converge.

So notice how you're living this last week before Christmas,
the preparations you make to meet your friends, to be part of your family,
to choose a gift to give, or a phrase or two to add to a card,
all of it is a little bit difficult isn't it.
Partly, we're pulled in the direction of meeting
some commercial standard of success,
and maybe for awhile we think we can manage it.

And then we have to acknowledge there is just so much we can do
to make everything perfect.
Same for the people who are in life with you: brothers,
parents, visiting friends, grandchildren,
they too are an unfinished story, and their lives and needs change,
just the way the ritual meals and customs change over time.

What can we do but remember that the unfolding of Christmas is God's doing.
And each day we can only listen and learn from one another.
Think of the week before Jesus' ninth birthday, or tenth,
or his eighteenth. That's the Christmas story too.
Those changes you've lived through but even yet, there's an expectation
of something altogether unexpected, purposeful, new.
And the goal is not so much a successful holiday, but rather to receive the love
that is risked in your direction, and to offer what you can in return.

We are unfinished, mysteries to ourselves, and yet grounded in hope.
I'd go so far as to say that is is at the very deepest center of life,
where things appear to be most unknown and perhaps most vulnerable
that the strength of Christ's presence, and God's purpose, is strongest.
Not our own answers for everything,
but Christ's own self, at the center, like the child carried within.

So religious faith, Advent faith, is strong, hopeful,
and also alert to much that we don't know and can't solve

Richard Bollman, SJ

and will always wonder about.
How do we connect to what God might even now be reshaping in us,
cleansing, replanting, pruning.
We connect by saying "Yes, be it done to me.
I am your servant, I am ready for what you want to accomplish in me."
This is Mary's prayer in Nazareth: be it done. Yes.

I came upon a passage from Thomas Merton
that helps me appreciate this inner place of mystery,
helps me to affirm its holiness and possibility.
He says (I paraphrase):
> There is something within us that only God can touch.
> It is untouched by illusion, lies; it is a point of pure truth,
> inaccessible to our fantasies and manipulation
> (how great we are, how awful)
> a point of absolute poverty.
> It belongs to God.

Merton calls it by a French expression, la point vierge—
the empty place, the virginal center.

And there are we in company with Mary this Advent.

3. STORIES OF CHRISTMAS

In a remarkable passage about prayer, Ignatius urges the contemplative practice of seeing the details of the events of Jesus' birth, in imagined detail, not research: the length of the highway, the number of people traveling, the size of the cave, the quality of light in darkness. It is an interior listening and appreciating what is wondrous and close, God among us, tasted and felt. It reminds me that people who come to hear about Christmas in Church are already involved in their own story of the festival, its struggles and its unusual openings to grace. Preaching at Midnight Mass becomes an invitation to share that sensed story of family, grace, and Jesus, welcoming everyone's presence, urging that they trust how Christmas might be happening again for all you who hear.

In this we find a way to remember who is here, to seek what we want, and to be part of the world in which God has become Flesh. Because of this birth, we dare not separate off from our bodies, our history and family, our desires, our relationships, our passions and mistakes, all those pressures by which we strive to be somebody, all the mistakes and the enrichment of loving. It is in this humanity that Christ has been born, and is being born.

Midnight Mass at Christmas
Isaiah 9:1-6; Titus 2:11-14; Luke 2:1-14

The scriptures of Christmas center on the announcement of Jesus' birth as told by Luke. This announcement is called "good news" for everybody, truly a privileged moment in the turnings of history.
But the Hebrew scriptures this evening are also crucial for our full understanding of the good news. For the hope of God's intervention in our struggles is much older than Jesus' time.

Isaiah's expectations were sung to a troubled people who lived in Jerusalem and the surrounding state of Judea about seven hundred years before Christ. Kingly leadership in those days frequently compromised the spiritual heritage of the people with unhealthy trade alliances, and these often led to danger from foreign invasion. Isaiah also realized that some of the fault lay in the people as a whole, willing to risk so much for material gain. He believed only God could restore a sense of security and integrity, and that God indeed would do this. God would inspire a new kind of wise leader. And it would be wonderful, like harvesters bringing in crops again, like an army burning the bloody boots and uniforms of the war dead because days of violence were over. We must listen to the prophet with eye and ear tuned to our own world where wise leadership and respectful foreign policies are still something to long for.

And there is also a word from the first century Jewish Christian Paul the Apostle. Though Christmas was not yet a festival celebrated by this early community, they had a deep sense of God's imminent coming among them in Christ, and this raised problems familiar to us all: how to live an authentic life of faith, in the midst of a worldly and very attractive commercial culture.

longing for home

HOMILY at CHRISTMAS, 1998

Earlier this month at a dinner for university Trustees,
there was entertainment by XU Singers,
a tenor and bass, soprano and two altos,
offering some carols in close harmony.

Their closing number was a pop favorite: "I'll Be Home for Christmas."
You remember: "you can count on me;
please have snow and mistletoe and presents by the tree."
It goes on: "Christmas Eve will find me where the lovelight gleams.
I'll be home for Christmas, if only in my dreams."

Selected Homilies

Well, I thought to myself, what sense do these kids make of this song,
that last line of poignant separation from home—only in my dreams.
If they happened to know the date on the song they'd get the picture: 1943.
These are the sentiments of a soldier in a USO canteen,
a marine in a Pacific army hospital. "I'll be home for Christmas" . . . if only,
and maybe not ever.
Christmas is a visit from Bob Hope maybe, and a brief respite
from firebombs and machine gun fire.

Yet the song is timeless.
Because our ideal Christmas, that sense of belonging, affection,
of giving and being gifted,
All this lives in tension and paradox with the harsher truths of family and society:
ruptured relationships, illnesses, blaming and back-biting among people,
fatigue, the mere stress of American holiday pressure,
the obvious contradictions of poverty and wealth so exposed in the marketplace,
and the pain of Church-going too. That pressure to belong in God's house
and our parent's traditions; but is this home for me?

I'll be home for Christmas, but does it mean I'll find God?
Often our souls aching is as serious a Christmas trauma
as bombs flying over London in the blitz,
or over Baghdad or Kosovo for that matter.
For the world's ache touches our own,
making every Christmas a new challenge of faith;
a challenge more stark because we desire so much of Christmas,
and we think we ought to have it, that it ought to sweep us up.
And if it doesn't, it's our own fault.

But the fact is, Christmas is hard to come home to,
and our idealization of it does not help.

The good news of faith is not "I'll be home for Christmas."
God does not promise us presents and snow and mistletoe: nothing like that.
God does not even say Merry Christmas: God says Jesus Christ.

Richard Bollman, SJ

Against the darkness of this night, and the anxiety of tomorrow morning,
God only says "Jesus Christ."

The theologians observe of Jesus
that he is God's last word on the problems we struggle with,
even our own sins.
And this last word is literally speechless, which is what "infant" means.
God's revelation is vulnerable with the weakness of any child,
and silent. Except for tears.
How amazing, that in our dark world
this is the light that has entered.

The journey of Christmas faith, then,
is to go right up against the darkness, right into it,
where we are simply not sure of our resources, perhaps even our survival:
to go right there in order to find
not solutions, but God's vulnerability in the dark with us,
and God's silence.

The Good News has to penetrate to these places, or what good is it?
I belong to a prayer group—we meet all too rarely,
but we meet before Christmas.
One of our members lost his father in death, a protracted illness,
a few years ago: and as we spoke a little
of what we'd like from God for Christmas,
he mentioned a few things about his children, and a stronger spirit of gratitude,
and then paused to add, almost matter of factly,
"I'd like to talk for awhile with Dad again."

That silence, which was suddenly a shared faith, palpable, almost a presence,
that's the Christmas place.
In such a moment, there is room for the Good News.

Let me tell you of a Christmas letter from my friend Margaret.
She was 32 when she married Joe, about 12 years ago.

Selected Homilies

He was a high school buddy of mine, 15 years older than she,
and the child they wanted never came, so they thought of adopting.
"At my age," Joe said, "it has to be Russia or eastern Europe–
conventional agencies are restrictive about age."
So they gradually made contact with 2, mind you, Russian boys,
one 4 the other 2, through several long flights to Moscow,
visits to orphanages, pictures and slow bonding and paper work,
and I thought–oh God, don't do it, man you're nearly 60–
and last Christmas I actually met the little kids. Alexsi,
the older, in the midst of a sudden gulp of American affluence
was turning into a wilful rambunctious bundle,
and in a kind of defensive posture chose to speak only the Russian he knew.
and Michail, manifested a wounded shyness nearly autistic.

But this year's letter held this news.
"Alex has mastered English–he thrives, he's grown 4 inches,
he is computer literate, so much more focussed.
Mike has begun to speak. Short sentences, yes,
one of them begins I want, and one begins No . . . .
But it is communication. And his personality blossoms–
he steals the hearts of his classmates in pre-school. He is known as the Hunk."

Then she speaks of herself.
"After 14 months, at least I can say that the thought of two small boys at home
is no longer a thrill or an anxiety. It is just a routine thought.
We have become a family of sometimes more, sometimes less cohesion."

That's it. In a year and a half, two small boys take slow steps to childhood,
and their adoptive mother finds something acceptable, matter of fact, very real
in the cost it has taken, and the rewards it has yielded.
Difficult rewards, don't you see?
Adult lives utterly changed forever. But that's okay.
Living in the gap, between what we expect
and what we find we are capable of, what love requires.
This is Christmas faith.

Richard Bollman, SJ

And finally, another Christmas letter, back to 1943.
Dietrich Bonhoeffer was a Lutheran pastor and theologian
imprisoned, eventually executed, for taking part in a plot against Hitler.
Prison was very harsh and foul, full of uncertainties,
and separation from his wife.
But in mid-December, he wrote to a close friend something about
his Christmas faith.

How his ministry and suffering have taught him
how much he loves life, and loves the whole earth.
And that it is only when all of that is threatened,
when even his enemies are threatened with the vengeance of God,
that he comes close to the sacred event of forgiveness,
which brings light into the the calamity. He finds that his instinct to forgive
is truly inspired by the forgiveness of God.

There it is again, I think,
the faith of Christmas taking shape in the dark and the silence,
a silence and a darkness that are no obstacle at all to what we really want,
but are almost the preconditions
for the Light of the World, to be born again among us.

Thanks also to YOU for venturing out this night to this place,
to make up the assembly of God.
What are we but an empty place where good news can happen.
Give up your plans for Christmas, and give up your apprehensions about God,
but go closer to the empty place where new birth is possible.
There you will find a baby, God who is speechless and new
and who is Jesus Christ, unfailingly with us in the silence,
yesterday, today, the same forever.

---

see Dietrich Bonhoeffer, *Letters and Papers from Prison*, pp 85-88

Selected Homilies

all you can buy

HOMILY at CHRISTMAS, 1999

Like you, I look for the good news of Christmas
in the midst of all we DO during the holiday time,
the preparations and visits.
I need good news as much as anybody.
Do you listen for it too?

Often enough it comes when you're not expecting it. In little visitations.
So it was only yesterday I met an acquaintance here,
a woman on the University staff, at morning Mass. I'll call her Karen.
She stopped deliberately after the morning mass to wish me happy Christmas,
and I did the same, and asked her: do you go away at this time?
Well yes, indeed she does;
and she spoke maybe seven or eight minutes
about what it was for her to go home, to meet Christmas there.

Home is a farming community in northern Ohio.
Her parents, Slavic immigrants, still host the whole family,
60 people when you count the guests,
at a kind of ritual Christmas dinner.
This has been Karen's Christmas as long as she can remember.
For the whole family, Christmas Eve is still a fast day (remember that old time?)
and the family sits down as dusk settles in
all at one table that their father sets up in a U-shape
in the big basement room, all decorated.
And there are prayers and blessings all through the ceremony,
sharing the first fruits of spring harvest and fall harvest.
Karen laughed: "these are small things, mind you:
spring harvest is cream of wheat, and fall harvest just beans and barley."

Richard Bollman, SJ

I asked about the center-piece: some big turkey, a goose?
"No," she said, "this is a very sacred meal, and vegetarian.
At the end we share some herring and tuna.
And then we all go off to midnight Mass."
That's when Christmas comes in, and the fast day ends.
"It's something," she said, "there are some toddlers,
who usually are held through the long parts of the meal,
or who mercifully drift off to sleep;
and there are the littler kids, antsy for it to be over,
and the teenagers rolling their eyes. But we're all there,
and each year I notice the college age nieces and nephews
bring home their dates, just to be part of this.
Guests are important: there's always one empty chair
filled only at the last minute with somebody in need, even a stranger."

I thought of my own family rituals,
a lot less focused on the religious meanings of Christmas,
and very changeable year to year, as generations move away
and form their own varying customs.
And I thought of what we really want as human beings,
a sense of belonging, knowing where home is,
and connecting that to our longing for God.
How wonderful it would be just to have that given us in an annual ritual that works.

For most of us, there isn't any farm to go home to,
and we've moved on into cities where there are more jobs
and greater chance of advancement,
even if that means moving every two years
from one metropolitan beltway to another.
This makes it hard for many people,
because community and contact with the sacred
are not commodities that you can buy.
We belong to an American way of life, not an old European tradition,
and though we have Christmas galore,
I hear from people that God is hard to find in the midst of it,
the good news grows faint.

Selected Homilies

So I left Karen, telling over to myself the details of her home visit,
as a vision of family and church and Christian life
that still works for people, gathers people, nourishes them,
somewhere on a farm north of here.
I felt closer to some kind of good news of Christmas
and wanted to do my own home visiting with more respect
for the gatherings that still happen, the rituals we do have.

Then today, as people were gathering just hours ago
for the Children's Mass at 4:30 here at Bellarmine,
just over there three rows from the back, I saw a couple I thought I knew.
They were early, waiting for things to get going.
So I worked my way down there and said
"don't I see you here now and then? Do you come often?"
"No, Father, unfortunately you don't see us often.
We just come each year to this Mass."
And the young man gestured to his aunt, who I recognized,
and I gathered she was his annual connection to Bellarmine.
"So you're in some other parish," I said, and he said,
"Well no, not exactly."
His wife, or girlfriend, plunged her hands down inside her coat
and shrugged a little and looked at the young man sideways.
He went on. "We really don't come anytime, except Christmas."

Oh, I thought, where to from here?
The question showed on my face. The young woman continued:
"I try one place or another;
during the summer I told myself I'd try harder. But it's just so boring."
A lot of theological truisms about faith and community and Christian life
came up in the back of my mind and seemed irrelevant to the moment.
For some reason, though, I wanted to continue talking
because I really liked this couple, their utter candor.
But I couldn't think of any next remark. I ended in some cordial way,
I think saying they're welcome any time they decide to come.

But in the several hours since, I realize that in them
I was closer to Christmas than ever.
Their presence brought the good news in.

Richard Bollman, SJ

All I could think of was that "for you, for you is born this day,
the Savior who is Christ the Lord."
Exactly in that honesty and quality of presence
and that being on the outside of business as usual in the Church.
I think of them, and will think of them often.
I wish I could convey to them how embarrassed I feel
that it is so hard for them not to be bored,
that Church gives them no sense of belonging,
few roots and little encouragement to grow as people.
Embarrassed that there were no rituals and tables here at Bellarmine
as rich and convincing as Karen's in her family's basement.
How embarrassed that we do so much
cautioning and teaching about life,
instead of plunging in with people to share the questions
and to celebrate where they ARE finding life,
where they're NOT bored.

I wish I had thought to tell them,
"today, this very night, you just may hear a whisper of good news.
Do not let any fear get in your way.
Take the news for yourself.
Christ is born for you, whether you come to Church or not.
Remember the shepherds. Did they change their lives? Who knows?
But they did feel surprise and fear and curiosity and ultimately joy.
They GOT IT, because in their poverty, they were ready.
Jesus said this over and over: God's kingdom is for you.
That's the simple truth, that's the good news."

The story is told of a monk in an old Greek town, a monastery,
who begged regularly in the town, and saved his coins for years,
out of a call he felt to visit the birthplace of the Savior,
to go to Bethlehem and walk three times around the basilica,
and to return home with that memory.
At last he had collected enough for frugal travel,
and he gathered some food and his coin purse
and he opened the gates and set out.
And before he had gone a long way from the enclosure,
he met a beggar at the town gates, an intent man, not very old,
who asked the monk where he was going.

Selected Homilies

"I'm going to Bethlehem," the monk explained.
"I feel I have a call to visit the birthplace of Jesus,
to walk around it three times, and to return with the blessing."
And the beggar only said,
"Do you have enough money for this journey?"
"Yes," the monk replied. "I've been saving for some years,
I have forty pounds by now."

And the beggar said to him:
"Well, you could do this. I have a wife and a young family,
and no work, little to eat.
I just beg while my wife cares for the children,
and we don't have much chance to break out of this.
But you could leave the forty pounds with me.
You could walk around me three times,
and go back to the monastery."
And this is what the monk did.
He set down his coin purse, reverently walked around the beggar,
as if he were walking around the holiest of shrines in the world,
the very birthplace at Bethlehem.
And he went back to the monastery, a changed man and radiant, because he knew
and believed he had seen Christ.

Happy Christmas to you too.

a christmas visitor

HOMILY at CHRISTMAS, 2000

Saturday, after a short and easy shopping trip on Ludlow
I stopped in to see a new release at the Esquire called

Richard Bollman, SJ

"You Can Count on Me."
You could call it a Christmas movie,
and as you drive home you may find yourself discovering the title of the film
as the second line of the World War II song "I'll Be Home for Christmas."
You see? It comes up naturally, you could probably all sing it.

So it's the story of a brother and sister now in their late twenties or early thirties,
and their effort to get to know each other, though their way of life is so different.
What's clear is their love for each other through this struggle,
and that their love cannot save them from often hurting each other.
That's what struck me as so true, how we just can't manage to love serenely,
because we're so different, even members of the same family.
This is a pain that is often very poignant at Christmas.

In the closing scenes, without giving it away too much,
Terry and Samantha, the brother and sister,
promise to remember each other always at Christmas;
and they also stay true to their differences, and their love.
It's hard to imagine anyone in the audience not remembering such reality
in your own life, feeling the honesty of it and the blessing,
as well as the desire it could be different.

But we're put here on earth to do two things, I guess:
one of them is to learn to love, to give love and receive it,
(and how absolutely precious that is, there is no way to live without it!)
And the other thing we need to do is find our own way,
listen to the calling inside, and be true to it.
In both these things we make very very many mistakes.
But there's no other way.

I remember once having a reunion, after nearly 40 years,
with the little girl I went to grade school with: call her Marian.
By a chance piece of luck I had found out
she was back in the states for a visit
from her current home which is in Sydney, Australia.
After a short visit with her mother, now 85, still alert and funny,
the two of us went to Biaggio's for lunch, also near the theater on Ludlow.

Selected Homilies

I found out that though we started out from such similar circumstances,
now her journey had taken her far from the Church,
following a kind of need to burst out.
She said, as early as grade school, she heard what the sisters told her,
but in some way didn't believe it.
"I tried to make it all work out," she said, "by entering the convent.
Two years I did that, then withdrew, finished Catholic high school,
and at college met the man I married."
It was with him that they found
new circumstances very far away, and where she has raised a family,
and works in a designing job with a textile firm.
She comes to mind because of the tension of life
that she has lived through with her mother and brothers and sisters,
the way differences and reconciliations have been part of it.
That mystery of love and yet following one's own path.

And what a thing for me to realize, that down the corridor in St. Clement's School
back in the middle nineteen forties, a little girl was listening to the nuns,
and something inside was saying she had to go a different way,
try as she might to conform!
I remember what Marian said to me,
when I asked her if she had any spiritual path.
She said, "I believe that if we're left to ourselves, and trusted,
we fundamentally will know what to do, and how to follow the right path,
and I think I've been doing that."

I felt very close to her in that conviction,
very much a brother to her, after all these years,
because in different ways, and with mistakes aplenty,
we'd each been following the path we could see and own up to.
That's the kinship I feel with many people I've met along the way
who don't call upon Christ, or who probably won't be in a Church tonight.
The thing I admire is the willingness to follow the path that invites them to life,
and to keep on loving the people who matter along the way.
I think of Marian as I hear the scriptures speak tonight
about the grace of God training us, demanding a lot of us.

Richard Bollman, SJ

She seemed to have been living a life, "eager to do what is right,"
as St. Paul says, "rejecting godless ways," ways where she found no gift nor life,
and going on to live temperately, justly, devoutly.

This is a strange Christmas sermon, you might think,
but I cling to the conviction that the incarnation is so important
that we have to trust the real truth of life, of how we're drawn,
what our passions teach us and what we learn from mistakes,
that sometimes even what our teachers tell us is not to the point
until we've lived a little.
And I trust it so much that I believe Christ will find us in the end,
will not let us fall away from his heart which is so strong for everyone,
which is Good News for all the people.

I wonder too, if in remembering Marian I'm not seeing clearly
the gift of my own faith, how it came alive to me not through words and sermons,
but through my talents, the people I loved and wanted to be like,
my restlessness, my fears and delays, mistakes and messiness,
the desires of my own heart for companionship and meaningful work to do.
So yes, this led me to the Society of Jesus, and to so many people who luckily
helped me to understand my calling at lots of different crossroads,
but I need to respect the desire that led Marian to the convent,
and out of the convent, to marriage and motherhood in Sydney, Australia.
And I believe that as I respect her story, I'm giving reverence
to those aspects of doubt and difference that are still a part of my own soul.

There are those good people who help us learn how to love,
and how to find our own truth at the same time, just by being so very different!
Maybe it's a clear difference, hard to break through,
like being of a different race;
or a distracting difference that can get in the way a while,
like knowing someone who is disabled, or whose suffering and distress
outstrip anything you've ever had to face yourself.
Maybe these blessed people live in our own family.

Yes, we sit at the same table, even this table tonight.
We even pray together, though it could be we're at odds about the names of God,

Selected Homilies

or the formalities of good liturgy.
How gracious God is to bring us together.
And gradually, we might be given the grace over the years
to see one another's goodness, even as we make mistakes in trying.

I left the Esquire on Saturday with a lot of tears,
and they wouldn't stop, because in half a block I passed the restaurant
where Marian had told me her story,
and all along up the street I walked pretty fast to get to the safety of my car.
You know the feeling, this kind of overflow, something hard to name
but a lot of your life is getting touched, some kind of strange reunion
with the essential truth.
And it might feel like sorrow, or longing, or joy, or forgiveness,
you hardly know what,
but at bottom I find more and more what I'm feeling is gratitude.
Just gratitude, that I'm alive at all,
that people are patient, and Christ is truly being born.

our night in Bethlehem

HOMILY at CHRISTMAS, 2002

One of the seasonal stories this year, tucked away in the national press,
concerns Bethlehem. I picked up on it in *America* magazine,
and *The New York Times*.

In 1995 the little town of Bethlehem was returned to the Palestinians
and there began a series of special Christmas celebrations in the square.
Both Christian and Muslim Palestinians, glad to have their city back,
were willing to notice their connection, their different faiths,
their need to live and share their world, their holy places,

Richard Bollman, SJ

and their hope for safety and nationhood.
Mr. Arafat, in those recent Christmases,
would come especially to the town's party,
to dramatize his role in this hope for a new national identity.
The residents of the town would be joined by thousands of tourists.
It would take an hour, waiting in line,
to gain access to the Church of the Nativity
and the small stone chamber which houses the place of Jesus' birth.

This year, the midnight Mass would have been celebrated just hours ago,
but there are no tourists in the town.
There haven't been for many months,
especially since the siege of April
when Muslim fighters took over the Church of the Nativity for 40 days
to hide out for safety. The events resolved in an uneasy peace for the town.
Then just a month ago, in retaliation for suicide bombings
that originated among the young Palestinians of the surrounding area,
Israeli tanks again have occupied Bethlehem.

The New York Times ran a picture of the interior chapel of Jesus birth,
a still and almost empty place, with stone floor and low ceiling.
There were only a dozen or so Franciscan nuns and friars in attendance.
The journalist quoted a wood carver, one Mr. Khano,
who said "there are no celebrations now, no festivals, only prayer."
Mr. Khano carves crib figures for a living, but sells nothing.
The tourist economy of the village has been stifled for a long time now.
But there is prayer, there is only prayer,
particularly among the Franciscans who were so instrumental
in alleviating the suffering of the besieged militants last April.
They work now pleading for humanitarian assistance
and offering help to Palestinian children who suffer from trauma.

Of course Christmas makes us sensitive to the sufferings of others.
That's one reason why these stories are around now.
But our concern for Bethlehem, and for the struggles of Israel and Palestine
is more than seasonal. It encroaches on our sense of well-being too,
as we try to steer through dangers on all sides

Selected Homilies

working toward some kind of more secure world.
Those dangers touch the hearts of people well beyond Christmas,
and well beyond Bethlehem.
We still have our festival and our visitors here tonight, but underneath
there is tension and dissent about the likelihood of war,
and there is a certain anxiety about jobs being downsized
and the economy under strain.

And wouldn't you think too that there is also among us
some silent place in front of the manger, where prayer is happening.
Pay attention to that prayer.

The wood-carver in Bethlehem seems to notice it,
maybe skeptically, maybe in hope. We should join in, and not disappoint him.
Picture this room empty for a moment of its accustomed festival.
Picture a slate floor worn by generations of tourists
now just bare and scrubbed and around the edge
a dozen or so nuns and friars of St. Francis,
letting prayer come forth from the hearts and voices.
It's easier to let our own prayer happen as we notice them.
And the wood-carver or some of the Muslim inn-keepers of Bethlehem
also join in, praying for tourists to come, for children to be safe.

We join them, couldn't we, for a few moments of contemplation
letting ourselves feel our own dangers and losses.
Among us, in our Christmas prayer, might be a reserve officer
called up for duty, a surprise beyond words;
or the parents of a young child abused by a priest they trusted,
and a college senior wondering about job interviews,
or the many among us broken by cancer, discouragement,
and the gradual dying of a spouse or a mother.
It's easier to let our prayer come to life as we bond with
the silence and the longings of other people.
Look around: the breathing network of humanity claiming faith,
it's here where good news starts to announce itself, heart to heart.
Your own dinner table might be that simple chapel of the birth place.
It cannot be all that distant from the original visitors to Jesus' cave,

Richard Bollman, SJ

who were the poor, and the criminal outcast groups,
coming in out of the night to see what might be possible
giving it all over to trust in the child now just born.
There is something essential here, that the light breaks in
upon the struggle of sorrow, and the experience of oppression.
Christ with us.

I was once a pilgrim in Bethlehem: it was nearly thirty years ago,
and Israel was well-guarded and the tour bus well managed,
again by the Franciscans,
and I traveled with my father and a Catholic pilgrim group.
Today I'd be afraid to travel there.
But I read that the Christians of Palestine long for tourists to come,
even in the face of danger,
and they remind us that pilgrims have always faced danger,
that this is the point of it: to risk all that you are
to arrive at the place of prayer with other pilgrims.
It's like building a new kind of world.

The Catholic Patriarch of Jerusalem declares
"we need a new type of pilgrim,
less like a tourist, one who comes out of conviction, who is fearless,
whose presence is a sign of hope for the three religions of the middle east."
I feel challenged by his words, to travel in my prayer and imagination
to the manger cave where so many sorrows of our church and world
start to move the hearts of people who need one another.
In such a place we are part of the same prayer,
for the liberation of ourselves, you and I,
and of all the world's traumatized people:
the children, the soldiers, our neighbors.
How good to be a fearless pilgrim toward
that kind of new place, in that union of faith.

Let us be touched then by today's town of Bethlehem,
and by the Bethlehem of Joseph, Mary, and Jesus.
We will find there no assurance of success, no escape from danger.
The streets of the town, whether Bethlehem or Over-the-Rhine,

Selected Homilies

might threaten us first before we find our way,
but then we meet other women and men, other faces and stories.
And it is all one prayer we are making:
you and I, and the jobless and the suspect,
those who have heard something, or who want to hear
angels telling good news.

For we all live in Bethlehem:
we meet there tonight.

this strange new birth

HOMILY at CHRISTMAS, 2004

I've always been an enthusiast for crib scenes.
I'm drawn to displays of them, big and small,
and I pay visits to churches to see how they do it up.
A dozen years back I acquired the creche you see displayed here,
but more to the point, I've hovered over it
micro-managing the placement and details
for every one of those twelve years since.
It's a way I do Christmas.

It goes back to boyhood: we had a small creche as I was growing up,
and it became my domain, my responsibility to put it under the tree.
My father handled the tree lights,
my mother and sister called out directions about the ornaments,
but I called the shots on the crib:
they were my actions figures, I'd devise stories about them,
and was acting out some needs in my imagination
to create a kind of anchor for Christmas in my family.

Richard Bollman, SJ

Or maybe I wanted a domestic atmosphere for myself
more serene than my real life,
with a devoted mother and father looking down upon the blissful boy.

We all have ways of doing this,
managing the details of our family situation
to make sure Christmas comes about in the right way.
Earlier today, one of our large parish families,
never so large as at Christmas,
were taking group photos by the icon up here:
they do it every year. It's a way of saying how they belong,
that they belong together, and belong here,
and the photo op makes it tangible.

The older I get, the more I know this kind of management
is impossible: as much as you'd like Christmas to be dependable,
even the same from year to year,
it changes, it gets away from you.
I finished the work on this year's crib arrangement around 12 noon today,
and had to sit down, with this funny feeling.
What was it, a kind of undertow of strangeness,
little scary apprehensions and wonderings?
It was as if some kind of Real Christmas might just plunge in upon me,
so different from the dreams we have about it.

I don't know who you will be assembling with tomorrow,
or what goes on in the effort it has taken you to be here now.
The important thing I find, as years change us,
is to allow for Christmas to find you fresh, to be different for you.
Which means we need to keep open to who people really are,
the real people, not the shepherds and saints and magi
who I am used to placing according to my creative imagination.
Just as we all tend to "place" each other according to our wishes!

For the real Christmas we live through,
though it sparkles with reunions, getting together, catching up,

Selected Homilies

is also a time when the losses in families are deeply felt,
the people who won't be at the table again. And that's as it needs to be.
Even new life in the household, the new son-in-law or grandchild,
wonderful as it can be, still demands a new kind of attention,
not always easy or welcome.
You may have come here tonight
with such a companion who has suffered a lot of change this past year,
or a daughter you feel you know less about after two years at college.
New things happening override our abilities to mange the scene.

So we're invited to allow for people to be different.
Maybe that's enough for me to offer of Good News this evening!
Allow for people to be different, let yourself listen,
see with new eyes, open up room for what's real.
That may be the whole asceticism of the feast.
To open your senses, hold your judgments,
lets you go down to the bottom of your love for the people you're with.

I know, after all, this is what we each need for ourselves in our own changes.
Because this undertow of strangeness, the funny feeling you get
in the dark night of Christmas itself,
it's partly the unfinished person you are yourself!

In the midst of an uncertain church, and an uncertain national purpose,
I have to admit I'm part of the uncertainty,
a human being with more questions than answers.
And here I am a Catholic besides.
How does that strike you, this year, I wonder:
what do you call yourself: a recovering Catholic, a sometime Catholic,
a believer, an inquirer, somebody looking for hope.
What kind of future is happening to us
as we ask our questions about lay leadership,
the shape and number of parishes to come,
the center of our life in the Eucharist, as priesthood declines.
How will we really see the possibilities coming up now
except by listening carefully to each other.
We are a Body being born.

Richard Bollman, SJ

A pastor friend of mine stirred my heart recently
telling how he stood in front of his congregation
wondering about the questions and lives and needs
especially of the young people there, the newly married,
the single young adults.
"I'm no longer sure where you are," he said.
"I thought I once knew. Can you take me to where you are,
and we can see it together?"

You might ask that question of your own children.
Can you take me to where you are, so we can see it together?
It is a question that certainly stays with me whenever I stand here,
and especially tonight, in the light of a birth we are always expecting.
We are a Body being born, called to a new place,
a people always strangely different from the expected.

So finally, when I set aside the effort of Christmas,
I come to realize that the funny feeling underneath
is actually a feeling of sorrow, sorrow for the lost Child I once was,
we all were—sorrow for the lost places and lost opportunities
that have fled away,
sorrow for the way things used to be, and are now so different.
And so there is nothing to do but to join in hope
for a new moment that is now taking place,
through every embarrassment about who we are and where we've been.

The strange and funny feeling is this: being invited to trust
the Word of God that has not yet found a voice,
a life among us that is holy, and so vulnerable to injustice and pain,
a creative birthing now into the future
that is nothing like where we used to be.
And it is already happening. Even as we take time
to look at the people we love, as they are,
to listen to the story they really want to tell,
and to take time to endure your own changes too.

Selected Homilies

And so you look at the Gospel, even at the crib, with fresh hope.
You feel your way with you hands, moving almost in the dark;
you touch someone's face, was it a shepherd?
or your good friend, or your son.
You trudge through the straw, or is it the discarded wrapping paper,
and you are inching your way to the mother and the baby,
and there does she look down into a face that is really your face,
as you are now, ready to trust, come what may.
And it is this face of the newborn that we seek this evening
and that we turn to one another.

We have a lot to live through yet, we who know this old story,
who believe that it tells our truth.
We are barely started. We are just being born.

Mid-Day Mass at Christmas
Isaiah 52:7-10; Hebrews 1:1-6; John 1:1-5, 9-14

**Following a very long tradition, there are three liturgies on Christmas,
each with its own scripture: one at Midnight, one at Dawn,
and this one now at mid-day.**

**The earlier masses tell the story of Christ's birth as given by Luke.
The Gospel you will hear now during this Mass comes from John,
a distinctive account of the origins of Jesus Christ
reaching back to the very first moment of creation.**

**The powerful divine nature of Jesus is also the subject
of the Letter to the Hebrews. This anonymous essay is an argument
about the superiority of Christ above all the religious figures
of the Old Testament, because he was indeed born before them.**

Richard Bollman, SJ

**We'll hear the opening verses of this Letter
which harmonize with what John has to say in the Gospel.**

**But first we listen to a poetic exclamation from the Prophet Isaiah
about the restoration of the holy community.
Listen to the tone of relief and joy at what is happening
to a broken and weary people. We believe that the gift of Christ today
is the fulfillment of our ancestors' enduring hope.**

the grace of the big bang

John 1:1-18

HOMILY 3rd MASS OF CHRISTMAS, 2016

Let's take this Gospel as the Christmas story for us this morning.
So it's as if John sits his listeners down and says, "now about Jesus
let's go back to the beginning, the first moments of creation.
In that moment when the dark world of nothingness trembled and exploded and suddenly there was light. Because God spoke.
That was the Word of God at work then."

And that has been the start of everybody's story.
This creative Word set into motion
a process of magnificent evolution and growth,
summed up in the phrase Light and Life.
And that goes way back in time beyond the little town of Bethlehem.

In our own day, we can look back through telescopes
looking into the past, and almost catch sight of that beginning.
Indeed that's what the astronomers are looking for: The Beginning!
It's a bit like what might tease your own thought when you look up,

Selected Homilies

and in a starry sky, or the darkness of that expanse, you wonder
about sources, meaning, origins. And we are finding something.
What we call the Big Bang is the emergence of something from nothing,
we can see almost to the first fire of that explosion,
seeing the light that has been traveling toward our telescopes
for 14 billion years.

And the amazing gift of human existence
is our ability to understand where we came from,
to feel it in our own bodies, and to say back: "thank you God
for this love which holds me together,
which knit me together in my mother's womb.
This growth that came through centuries of development
to the elements from which we are also made:
hydrogen, carbon, oxygen, blood, water, bone."
As the cosmologists like to say, it's all stardust,
we are made of stardust. Which is to say,
we are children of that first creative word.
And that Word became flesh and dwells with us now.

Dwells with us in a coherent array of continuing explosions and dyings,
orbiting together, held together. Indeed, why did it not just blow apart?
How did the Word of God keep everything at one with itself, all that is made?
What we notice is often called just 'gravity' a law without formula,
and without any rational explanation.
A cosmologist I value compares it to allurement, love even,
that mystery that holds us together, that encourages things to last.

So this is the prayer I recommend in the season now, this coming together:
that you can say to one another
I belong here, I was created to be here, thank you.
I belong to this world, I belong to you my God,
to you my friend who loves me, sitting next to me, we belong.
I am sister and brother of Jesus
and in him we've all been made alive and have been given light to see.
Our lives are following those same laws of light and love
that pulse through the whole cosmos.
Love loving us.

Richard Bollman, SJ

I have a friend who wrestles with her humanity especially at Christmas,
She tells me in a letter how she yearns again
for that ideal family she will never have,
and wishes for companions in her faith,
but her friends have turned away from religion.
It's a dark time, and she knows the triggers of this darkness,
the childhood wounds, even the diagnoses through the years,
and she trusts me enough, one more time, to just lay it out.
And finally she claims one thing of value, her love for her children.
The word made flesh. There she feels it,
a movement of love, the way the stars feel gravity, it gets her grounded.
Here she belongs. Here she sees how God works with her,
and how human growth and coming to peace,
well it takes a long time.

When I was a child, I was very taken up with crib scenes,
the big one in St. Clement Church, the small one we had at the house,
and that big life size one that's over in Eden Park now.
This scene just got to me, and it still does.
As an adult now I see: this is not as a sign of a past event,
but as a sign of God's nearness to us. And to me.

God near to me in the stardust from which I was made,
and in all my physical changes, wherever I sense my life this morning.
This is the closeness of God, the word made flesh.
Near to us, our flesh, our bodies and lives. Our breathing.
As near as the hand you hold,
as near as your own children,
as near as your aging body with its anxieties and questions, in that mystery, where
we know the darkness and the hope of living.

Thank you for coming this morning, for making it more real,
the Body of Christ, this assembly.
We are sisters and brothers of the Word of God.
This Child abiding with us is our origin, our inheritance,
our deepest valuing of life.

"From his fulness we have, all of us, received, grace upon grace."

Selected Homilies

The Celebration of Epiphany
Matthew 2:1-12

Matthew offers the other story of Jesus' birth, telling of the family living in Bethlehem from the start, Jesus about two years old, and a discovery of his arrival through the star, rather than angels. It is an event for the world at large, from the beginning, politically threatening to the royal family of Herod, but attractive to learned inquirers from that vast other world, "the east." It evokes a story of wonder.

the story of herod

Herod sent the magi to Bethlehem and said,

"Go and search diligently for the child. When you have found him, bring me word, that I too may go and do him homage." (Matthew 2:8)

HOMILY at Epiphany, 1995

Herod the King is a key player in this story.
He interests me.
Wherever there are seekers, visionaries, astrologers,
looking for the simple presence of the divine child,
there are other forces that resist, shrink back,
hold on to their security, want no rumors of God.

Richard Bollman, SJ

We know a lot about Herod
from the first-century historian, Josephus.
He started his career at age 25, at the behest of his father,
as the strategic on-site commander of Galilee.
He was known for his vigor, intelligence, and ambition.

In the following ten years he became
a veteran of political maneuvering,
during all those shifts in Roman power
that followed the assassination of Julius Caesar.
You read about this in Shakespeare and classical literature.
Herod was biding his time while Anthony wooed Cleopatra.
He visited Rome twice, befriending the political survivors,
and was appointed King of Judea in 37 BC. He was 35.

Part of the bargain was his promise to rid the Romans
of the previous ruler Antigonus. But Antigonus
was also a family member, an uncle of Herod, I believe,
so that Herod's rule needed to be secured through the years
by family purges: wives, brothers-in-law.
He was constantly rewriting his will.

But this man died in his bed.
After a life of reasonable success as a power broker,
after a few good public works projects
and more than a little violence and self-indulgence,
he died in his late sixties, a few years after Jesus was born.

He would have been 65 when the Magi arrived at his court
with the awful news of the child King,
the messianic hope, the new era.
A threat of change in Herod's arrangements.

Selected Homilies

And he decided to resist.
It is ironic: for it is precisely for the sake of
the Herods of this world that Jesus is important.
For those who dwell in darkness, the light has come.
Surely a man like Herod could use some light,
some deeper wisdom in his life,
some healing or reconciling grace:
but is it not welcome.

He reminds me, in rough outline, of Boris Yeltsin
engaged this Christmas season in a no-win policy
of suppressing Chechnian resistance fighters.

This weekend, the Russian orthodox Christians
hold the most solemn days of their Christmas
remembering the star, the Magi who followed it,
and the light that has come.
Last night the TV cameras visited
some of those gold-domed holy churches;
The incense was smoking,
and outside some citizens spoke in interview
of their distress at the death of the innocent,
and the disgraceful loss
of so many of their own young soldiers.

It was as if the light was coming into their own souls
saying things in criticism of policy that showed
a little of the new democratic climate.
But the light does not penetrate public policy.
And we mourn for our lost children
and our suffering old people without homes.

These things are not far from our national experience,
our own questionable policies and security,
both now and in the recent past.
I confess it is easier to point out Yeltsin,

Richard Bollman, SJ

and to claim a kind of mere confusion about things at home.
I don't want to be political here.

Yet for those who dwell in darkness, the light has arrived.
The new-born presence: Jesus, always new,
always arriving, dawning, in our thoughts and hopes,
bumping up against our self-protective maneuvering,
here to make a difference.
Isn't that a stretch to the imagination!
What do you make of it?

Ah, Herod, old man, why didn't you
join the astrologers that night, yield up your prerogatives,
relax your grasping old heart at last
to make that simple journey with them.
Why didn't you surrender to the lure of the star,
or catch the ardent yearning of those who could see it.
What were you afraid of? How this child might
captivate you, heal you, transform you?
Had you become so numb to your own needs?

Indeed, what do we all hold on to
that impedes our approach, this most basic gesture,
to be in the presence of the one who has come,
to be captivated, healed, transformed.
What lies, preoccupations, reasonable doubts, resentments,
disallow the light of this child
from melting our own old ways
and warming our souls
with the simplicity of his radiance.

What do we hold on to so tightly,
doing violence to our own hearts,
when his arrival is really what we want.
Do we think that we are not worthy?

Selected Homilies

or that this child and his mother and all the saints
have no notion of our longing?

It is still Christmas.
Surrender. Entrust yourself.
Open your treasure.

consider the magi

HOMILY at Epiphany, 2004

Let's say we know more about these magi than we really do.
Let's work our way into their story.
Because, after all, this is a story of searching
and of desire that continues to happen.
The searching, the desire, it is part of ourselves too.
So let's say we can use our imagination about them.

Let's say one of the magi came all the way from the Indus River
which runs north to south through Pakistan; and he was a Hindu mystic;
and again one of the magi came down from Armenia near the Caspian Sea,
and this was a woman magus, leader of a mystery religion, a local cult,
who was intent on finding something more universal,
more consoling for her spirit;
and then a third magus came from Babylon itself,
and he was a Jew, descended from a family who had lingered after the exile,
and he made a living interpreting dreams,
and he traveled with his whole family.
The three of them have been following the star from its rising.

Richard Bollman, SJ

And after individual journeys they met in a caravansary, let's say,
along a well-traveled road south from the Caucasus,
and gradually west toward Jerusalem.
They became acquainted because they were following the same star.
It was at the caravansary that they spoke of it,
and became aware that they were part of the same search.
And they could see good reason to team up,
to lighten the burdens of travel.
Their days would go like this:
they would start early before the sun rose,
while the star was still clear, just a hint of color washing around it,
and they would move in the cooler air, until the midday heat
suggest they have a lunch break of figs and pickled fruits,
nutmeats and water, until in the evening, at an oasis or larger hostel
they would have a larger meal from their stores and bed down for the night.

Those nights, after they came to know one another,
they would talk about the journey.
Imagine them under the desert sky.
They would first plot the course of the star,
because they all had their star lore, their maps.
But then, as good travelers, let us imagine they would come, after while,
to speak more personally, what the star was coming to teach them,
what the journey was coming to reveal to them.

One night, the learned and holy man from India said this:
"Because of this journey with the star I find I am becoming a man of prayer.
I mean a man of a new kind of prayer for me. As if for the first time.
No longer do I spend the day with my prayer beads asking for things.
This has all gone by the way. Instead I see that each day
my prayer is nothing more than to become aware of
my place in the caravan, my place under the stars, my place in reality.
That is all it is: a whole life of prayer just appreciating my place in things.
So each day my prayer is getting up before the first rosy streaks of light emerge
around the star, and each morning,
my prayer is adding dry grass and dung to the fire embers
so we can have our tea and boil lentils and fry the bread.

Selected Homilies

This is my prayer, being aware and alive to everything.
And each day more and more I refrain from judging badly
the snores of my servants over supper,
and each day in the heat I allow my sweat smells
to mingle with the camel smells, and I feel a great peace.
I think my prayer is very calm, like a lake reflecting the stars at night.
I think I am learning this from the star itself,
from this light that is coming."

And that is what the holy man said,
what he was receiving and savoring from the journey.
And on another night, the woman spoke.
She said, "With this journey I am finding out something.
I am discovering that I have confidence as a traveler.
I am discovering my own strength. I didn't know whether this would come.
I have never taken risks like these.
I have had some success in life, but it has always been called Luck,
or it has always been the result of doing the ritual the right way.
But now I have an actual light to follow. Now I am secure
because I look to a new kind of guidance that is beyond my understanding.
And it is wonderful to feel this security.
I think I can follow this light even through a dust storm
because I am finding in my deepest soul a connection to this guidance.
A kinship. I know the light will always be there."

That is what she said, the woman spiritual leader from Armenia.
And as they were getting close to the heights above Jerusalem,
that night as they prepared for sleep, the Jewish magus
talked about his journey.
He said, "This whole trip has become an occasion for me
to learn how to love my family, how to talk with them and open to them.
I never had to do this: there would always be my work,
and the children's teachers,
and the custom of community which separates men from women,
and at most I would talk with them about their grades in school,
or I'd talk with her about her cousin's better job,
or I would share some gossip and then just get angry.

Richard Bollman, SJ

Now each night we speak of life itself,
we remember the days of courtship and childbirth,
and we tell the children stories of our ancestors,
and listen to their questions and their hopes.
I feel it is connected to a Messiah that is right at our doorstep,
and that I can finally return to my roots.
I think I am already returning to my roots because I am finding such affection for my children, even my daughters,
and I am returning the affection my wife has always had for me.
I have this great thankfulness, and all because of this journey, this star."
Each night they would speak of these things,
as the sweet evening breezes brought their travel day to an end.

Can't you imagine travelers like this, magi like this, searchers:
a religious man discovering a new simplicity in prayer
just living in the moment;
or a woman becoming a confident traveler,
trusting that there is guidance for her
that she doesn't have to explain or attribute to luck;
can't you imagine a family man on the journey learning simply
to yield more toward affection and gratitude
in his day to day responsibilities.

These are the gifts they received as they went their way.

Are these the magi who actually made the trip?
Or are these good people—just ourselves?
What is it like for you to live in the light that has come now.
What is the gift of Christmas for you, the gift of life for you right now.
What awareness and alertness to the moment,
what confidence in your journey,
what new gratitude and affection for your closest friends.

Christ is light. The light that comes.
Whether or not we find a child near Jerusalem,

Selected Homilies

Epiphany is what matters most, the Revelation of this Light as it comes upon each of us.
The light that is coming to you. It is worth everything.
Once you come to trust it, you will never be the same.

Richard Bollman, SJ

4. MEETING JESUS

The Gospels, and almost all of the New Testament, unfolds gradually through a year of Sundays, and even then it's unfinished. The best of our experience allows that there is always more to take in, and more of ourselves to yield to the presence of this one Jesus. His being revealed, shown to us, this is that deeper sense of what Christian life is really about, someone to come to know and love, not just rules or traditions to follow. And our own stories, opened up and continuing, are touched by what we read, as if we come upon, Sunday a week or a month or year older, and so what we hear and hope for keeps evolving. It is always a more complete revelation of Christ. And it guides our own story, offering hope and direction, persevering in this even in the struggle of his arrest and death.

Consider first then the newness of that arrival, directed toward us, the possibility of being changed, walking the path with assurance and even a kind of joy.

who he is among us

THE BAPTISM OF THE LORD, B

It happened in those days that Jesus came from Nazareth of Galilee and was baptized in the Jordan by John. On coming up out of the water he saw the heavens being torn open and the Spirit, like a dove, descending upon him. And a voice came from the heavens, "You are my beloved Son; with you I am well pleased." (Mark 1:9-11)

*Here is my servant whom I uphold,
my chosen one with whom I am pleased.*

Upon him I have put my spirit;
he shall bring forth justice to the nations.
He will not cry out, nor shout,
nor make his voice heard in the street.
A bruised reed he will not break,
and a dimly burning wick he will not quench. (Isaiah 42:1-3)

HOMILY

This account of the Baptism of the Lord concludes the Christmas season,
making it clear that the essential beginning of the story,
is not merely the birth of Jesus, but the revelation of his significance.
Probably the story we hear today, the baptism of Jesus,
is the oldest such revelation story, and it is told by each of the Gospels.

Listen to it then: the voice of God is the "First Noel,"
the first revelation of Jesus as the good news of God.
The child we found is now the adult making this venture,
and finding God with him.

Let's reach back a little farther, to that point in time where Jesus left home.
He had no disciples, no public reputation.
If any shepherds from thirty years ago recalled his birth,
they have forgotten it by this time.
If any rabbis or lawyers who met him when he was twelve
still recalled that day, they have left no indication.
That was eighteen years ago.
As John the evangelist says,
he was in the world, and the world did not know him.
As John the baptizer said,
there is one among you who is powerful,
and he is coming, and he must increase.

Richard Bollman, SJ

And then something prompted Jesus to leave home
and to take a ninety mile walk to the region south of Jerusalem
where John was baptizing.
Because, of all that was going on in Judaism,
John attracted Jesus' attention.
John had no plans for overthrowing Roman occupation;
he had no role in the Jewish religious leadership;
he had only a simple message about God's closeness,
and the powerful anointed of God being very close,
and that everybody was welcome to come out for this.

And everybody was coming! The learned among the Jews
were interested in John and interrogated him about his intentions.
The common workers and soldiers were concerned about being included
in the new approach of God that John announced,
and they would ask about how to behave.
People were persuaded to come into the water,
to be made ready, to be cleansed and to be marked as new,
to come through to the new community.
You have to believe, then, that there was a hope in the air,
and a felt need for God's intervention, even though
nobody could guarantee how to make that happen.

But John was a man who could help a crowd of mixed people
realize something of what they themselves wanted:
things not too different from what we want lately.
An end of untruth and hypocrisy in high places,
an end of confusion and feeling like second class people,
a new burst of Spirit power, such as had marked the people of Moses,
and the kingship of David,
and the prophets who brought the exiles back to a new order of Jewish identity.
John tapped something real: that all God's people
might be spirit people, might be powerful,
because of the great power of the one who is coming among us.

So in that time of expectation,
an obscure thirty-year-old stepped into the water with everybody else,

Selected Homilies

and God chose him, elected him, singled him out,
called him the beloved: opened the heavens above him.
By this John knew what he needed to know: that Jesus had arrived.

The revelation that God announced at this moment in history
was not a detailed scheme of theology nor a new set of 10 commandments.
The revelation was the person of Jesus. The person himself.
And the Gospel stories, one after another, are preserved and arranged
so that by listening centuries later
we can come under the influence of this Jesus.

It is not so much what he says or does that affects us now,
but it is who he is: the person who speaks and acts,
this is the mystery to get close to,
to be influenced by:
how he has faith in people,
how he identifies the evil spirits and rebukes them,
how he acts without fear of persons, and without violence,
how he loves people as they are and leaves them
better than they thought possible,
how he empowers them—
all this is the way the good news happens in this world.

We learn Christ from within, by the influence his presence begins to have.
That's how he affected those he met
and that's how he continues to affect Christian congregations.
We start to understand our holiness then
not by how much we know or how long we pray,
but by the way our presence, affected by who Jesus is,
helps people to trust themselves and choose good;
that is a holy person, one who raises the self-esteem and spirited peace
of the people he or she encounters.
The influence of Jesus, shared through our encounters,
begins to cast out fear,
the fear of failure, being tired or discouraged, even dying,
because all of this is the human life Jesus knows and feels good about.

Richard Bollman, SJ

To meet Jesus is to begin to change.
To meet Jesus is to begin to realize our own capacities to love,
to see other people, to be free of our addictions, to expel the demons,
and to long for the justice of God: that harmony of purpose
that we start to have almost direct knowledge of.

I had an good example of this sort of thing just last Tuesday
at an open session with the new superintendent of schools, Alton Frailey.
Everybody there had a keen interest in schools and education
and a need for improvement, growth, honest accountability.
But mainly what people wanted was to get to know this man:
and he placed himself clearly there,
talked of his conviction about belonging in the job,
said through many images and stories that he likes to work in dialogue
and that he is action oriented,
and that his bottom line interest is the child, the education of our real children.

He gathered agreement as he talked,
and a sense of appreciation started to grow in the room.
I believe this happened not just because of the quality of the man
but because of the qualities in the people who listened, what they all brought,
how some common conviction and power was being called out,
and it could affect our schools and ourselves for the better.
It would have been that way with the Baptist: a spark, an interaction
between John's convictions, and the felt needs of those who came.

This is not to say that Mr. Frailey is exceptionally Christ-like,
though he does have many fine qualities.
It's to say that he has faith in a very deep life and goodness
that is possible in people, and that this was an occasion, a simple one,
where there was the hidden Christ revealed among us
the one we are coming to know,
who is more powerful than any of our own individual agendas,
and more powerful than our single efforts.

Selected Homilies

We share an age of expectation, an era of dire threat and great hope,
we form a church pained at its hypocrisy and convinced
that there is still a powerful Christ to be revealed.
We stand at a point of risk, to come under Christ's influence,
open to that relationship, and to faith-filled contact with one another.
This is where we are, this is who he is,
here as we listen.

knowing what to do

3rd Sunday, B

After John had been arrested, Jesus came to Galilee proclaiming the gospel of God: "This is the time of fulfillment. The kingdom of God is at hand. Repent, and believe in the gospel." As he passed by the Sea of Galilee, he saw Simon and his brother Andrew casting their nets into the sea; they were fishermen. Jesus said to them, "Come after me, and I will make you fishers of men." Then they abandoned their nets and followed him. (Mark 1:14-18)

HOMILY

Picture this now,
the broad surface of the Sea of Galilee,
the color of turquoise, a vast lake you can see across,
but not very far down, never all the way down.
The broad surface of the water, picture it
under the bright, dry air of Judea probably toward the end of the day.
It is net-mending time, a moment for a last catch from the shallows,

Richard Bollman, SJ

shore work.
So the sun would slant in from the west, onto the water;
the sky opposite the shore a most intense blue.
The arc of the last net cast out drops a spray that sparkles.

The arc of the net, cast wide:
this itself gives Jesus a sense of his moment,
the reach, and the abundance of the gathering in.
"Now THIS is what my life is about,
this moment, this richness, the lake full of fish.
And more than that. Skilled workers of this kind,
able to balance in the boat, not too tired for a closing catch,
this kind of person, this moment of gathering in,
will make clear to everyone the fundamental good news–
God's power is close and full and ready now in this world."

Of course there would be contrary voices inside Jesus:
he had heard them before.
"You belong to a small vassal nation subject to Rome,
at the margin of the empire;
you stand in a religious tradition dividing into factions;
and yes, life is abundant, as long as you're not a leper,
or approached by demons, or a widow.
In the world around this shore line
powerful dark forces are at work, and you are small;
you could not even manage a boat in the center of the lake,
or call up convictions in men so different from yourself.
Count your troops, assess your needs,
and if you're going to do something to help,
you'd better be sure to figure out exactly what it is–
turn stones to bread, maybe."

He'd heard such voices before, and knew where they came from,
and he set them aside.
For here the truth was plain,
it caught his eye and his heart at once.
A fish-net cast wide,

Selected Homilies

and under it two brothers balancing easily in the boat,
instinctively and without thinking, throwing their arms way out
with life about to burst forth from under the water.
That is it; the moment of God, its true vitality,
its harmony and opportunity.

"Repent and believe this good news."
He said it to himself again.
And then he said to the brothers,
"Follow me."

What happened to them in that moment,
that hearing, that realization of what to do now?
Something almost electric, a turn, an innovation, and utterly simple,
simple as letting go of the net.
That is what they felt, their hand free of the wet cords,
and with that felt release,
a recognition of one who had called them,
as if Life itself had spoken,
and the whole day came together,
now not just a routine of toil and counting,
day after day catching and selling,
but something different:
a network of human beings, a gathering in,
and an aspiration within them even to let God be God,
feeling the abundance of the lake to be more than itself finally,
a sign of something enormous about the world, about who to trust.

"The time is now, step into this moment when God is completely in charge,
follow where you are led, listen to this voice and the promise in it;
and everything else is a minor matter,
whether you are married or unmarried, mourning or joyful,
wealthy or poor.
Let everything go and follow the holy Child of God
who is inviting you to see the true work that life calls you to.
Drop the net lightly and listen."

Richard Bollman, SJ

This moment, such a moment of Good News, the kairos of God,
this is never exhausted, never old, never over and done with.
It is now, wherever you are in your own toil.
In the teaching you do, or the managing,
the twins born last month, pulling the family into new friendships,
the sorting out of personal issues, the buying or selling, or the gardening,
or the volunteer board membership, or waiting for a job offer . . . . .
You can live that moment partially, doubtful,
rueful, calculating and resenting and thinking hard,
worrying and burdened by routine.
Or, you can let Jesus look at you, notice this invitation,
and see through to what you really want to accomplish:
the gathering together, healing, loving
that is even now waiting to come alive in your moment,
your heart's desire.

God is powerfully at work in this world.
And the power of God is always now.
Repent and believe this good news,
and as that grows powerful in us,
the strength of doubt, and the willful destruction of life
so strong around us in the world
begins to weaken and recede from our imagination
and lose its power.

We can simply let go of our nets, to trust what life wants to offer
from the heart of the moment.
I speak of a specific relationship we have
with the Christ of God; each of us.
I'm reminding you of the faith we profess,
that we are never far from the Kingdom of God.
You are where you are in order to
let God make a difference through you.
Give yourself.

Could we even do this in our parish life,
our efforts to gather and choose and network:

Selected Homilies

hold it lightly, listen deep,
and trust the life that wants to come.
That would be worship, the offering, the reality of it,
on this Sunday, the one we have.
And each week. How it could move and hold us all!

salt and light

5th Sunday, A
Matthew 5:13-16

Matthew's inaugural discourse from Jesus, the first of five sermons, is also the longest. It began a week ago with the eight sayings about human happiness and our connection to the Kingdom of God. The very next passage affirms who he believes us to be, and how he trusts us to matters, as salt and as light. It is an encouragement toward presence to one another, human beings in touch.

HOMILY

Some passages of a Gospel are so short
you have to find people to talk to. It's beyond study and footnotes.
Salt and light, I thought, happens in conversation, encounter.
It was 10 a.m.
So I swept the snow off my car and drove up to the main campus
and stopped in on the adult education session.

The topic was Compassionate Listening,
but more to the point, the presenter was offering a chance to listen together,

Richard Bollman, SJ

and consider what we mean by salt and light. A dialogue on the scripture.
I was with three parish members in the breakout group,
all of them married, fathers of families
(whose children were in classes down the hall).
We asked, is light something your are supposed to DO,
(we thought not) or is it something we ARE, as human beings
(and that seemed true), and the important deal
is to let human beings have time to venture
even past their initial fear of shyness, or disagreement.
Or fear even, or anger, so that light can be recognized, be present.

It was a brief time, but we were willing to speak of
places in life where conversation is difficult, where compassion
can be blocked by defensiveness (the bushel) with a friend, or fear to venture.
And I thought of a conversation I had had earlier this week
where my own light flickered to near zero because I was not able
to see past my apprehension of disagreement, and so I ended up
with less life and love for another than I might have found.
It makes me hungry, once again, to be who I am in a risky encounter,
To even ask: "can we slow down: I'm not sure where I am right now."
Has this ever occurred to you? So it was in the small group.
I saw a piece of my life more openly now.
I realized I don't need to hide as much as I do.
I don't have all the light there is, but I do have some!

So then, I went back to my house for breakfast,
very glad that I had taken time away, because the point of the Gospel
declares something important about the nature of the faith community,
how we are called to be engaged together. How light comes
from a willingness to spend it, give time to it,
how seasoning comes from our presence, when we do trust ourselves,
when we know we are salt, and can expect seasoned mutuality
when we listen and open our desires.

I think of this whole teaching summed up in a phrase I heard
from a Jesuit speaker, Pat McGrath was his name, a few Lents ago.
Talking about his own story, he pictured Jesus saying:

Selected Homilies

"What if I were to show you more deeply your own life,
and what I love about you?" The salt and light!
That feels to me like the voice of Jesus within these teachings.

I thought back to the Gospel a week ago:
Blessed are you, poor in spirit, open and hopeful,
and so there is more room for Me to be with you:
Blessed are you in sorrow, allowing your tears,
searching for God's way of life, longing for peace,
listening to one another, fathers and friends,
able to care for one another. Seasoning for me.
Let yourself have the joy of encounter, just jump in.
Let your light be shared, falling upon the hearts of your friends,
or strangers, trust it to awaken a desire for more.

"What if I were to show you more deeply your own life,
and what I love about you?"

I remember another wintry example, even though it was April
last year on my slow sabbatical crawl up around Michigan,
driving along through the very slow spring,
snowy and grey, tracing the UP shore of Lake Michigan,
down into Ste. Ignace, (above Mackinac) the Budget Host Inn.
Early Jesuit territory, I realized, Marquette country.
And after I settled in, I asked the genial Budget Host himself
where to find dinner. White fish?
"Oh yeah," he tells me, "well the season isn't quite open,
but there's a big all purpose diner down toward the town,
they ought to have white fish."

The diner looked unpromising from the road, but the town itself
had a certain appeal even in the chilly grey, with dusk coming on,
a line of shops and exhibits, mostly closed, to the right,
and the harbor and shoreline of Lake Huron to the left.
And one tourist store was open, The Pavilion, where I bought
some wine glasses for the vacation cottage where I'd be the next day,

and the owner offered free coffee in exchange, good coffee,
and a long story about Lake Huron, that fine world of summer sailing,
because unlike Lake Michigan there are lots of small islands to set out for,
and many little ports and horizons, and how once he and some friends
faced 24 foot waves out there, and. . . . "well yes, there is good white fish
up at the bowling alley, just down past the shops and turn right up the hill."
And so it was. I could find it in the dark.

And in the bowling alley, there was lots of light, and an open place at the bar
where the locals were enjoying their white fish and beer.
From inside my own soul some voice said, "Well, I guess there's room here."
And I took the seat. The couple to my right knew the Pavilion shop owner,
and I told them I was a traveling Jesuit,
and they spoke of the Marquette museum, closed in the off season,
but a good one: and the man to the left was a salesman
from Traverse City, whiling away the evening now,
so glad that Ste. Ignace was still in the off season, the quiet,
a real break from his work. He told how Traverse City
was once small and quiet, just one main street along the shore line,
before it expanded with tourists and miniature golf and fast food.
I felt so engaged, so full of talk. The fulness, the gift, it amazed me.

And so, on my way back to Budget Host Inn I pulled off the main street
to a long parking pier, got out, and shouted for joy into the blustery water,
and began to sing a song. Something of happiness, of blessedness.

"What if I were to show you more deeply your own life,
And what I love about you!" The salt and light.
Wherever we venture, and stand in the clear, God shall find us
and let us know who we are. We need not hide. Such an engagement.
It will overflow.

What if I were to show you!

Selected Homilies

invitations

5th Sunday, C
Isaiah 6:1-8; 1 Corinthians 15:1-11; Luke 5:1-11

Luke's Gospel, still in the beginning chapters, tells the story of the calling of the first apostles, the familiar fishermen, Peter and James and John. In Luke's account, there's a little psychology in the event, a weighing of the implications. Like with Moses, for example, or Jeremiah or Mary Mother of Jesus, there's a moment of hesitation, questioning. And there is a parallel in the calling of Isaiah. Like Peter, Isaiah hesitates because he feels unworthy. Then in the Letter to the Corinthians, Paul talks about his own calling, in the context of meeting the risen Jesus. He too is aware of his sinfulness, a matter that does not get in the way of his being fruitful and confident.

HOMILY

So we have three roughly parallel figures here,
Paul, Peter, and long before them, Isaiah,
who tell of having an encounter with God: something of great impact--
the risen Jesus stepping into your path, or a vision in the temple,
hearing a voice, seeing signs of great power: angel wings,
or this overflowing of fish in the boat.

What do we take from this? It's the core of our faith, really.
God intervenes in human affairs, nudges us, speaks to the heart,
shows us that we can trust God, or Jesus,
to bring direction into our journey, life, involvement.
Take this in a moment, how it happens, how it attracts a person, what we want!

Richard Bollman, SJ

And to be sure, stories of this kind emerge
among the women of the Bible too: Ruth, Mary, Mary Magdalen,
callings and changes that affect the direction of the community:
messages from angels or from life itself, suddenly making a turn.
Indeed, these nudges and indications come
in the most ordinary flow of our life, our basic routines.
Paul was just following his routine, part of the collective regime,
political and religious prejudice was part of it;
Isaiah was doing his temple duty,
Peter was cleaning out the boat.

How do these things happen, that we get spoken to, launched in life.
Rilke, a German lyric poet, has said simply:
"God speaks to each of us as he makes us."
Our own make-up, our history, our talents as we find them,
this is sacred ground. Our being made, as we are made,
this is the word to us, the presence.
At any stage of life, really.

Skill is part of it. Good basketball players have a kind of agility,
a certain caginess about finding open spots, bodily flexibility,
strength and speed . . . you stay with it. You'll do well.
Or you might say of a young woman, she really speaks to the point,
and she has a mind that can handle lots of facts without losing her way.
She is able to see the importance of tradition and custom,
and yet she has a passion for the rights of people who are held down.
Maybe she would make a great defense lawyer. A congresswoman.
God speaks to each of us as he makes us.

And along with our talent, there is a person's felt sense of passion.
You weigh these things in the crucible of your own enthusiasm.
Vision comes when you're fully alive, with your eyes open.
It's all miracle, all gift. And I'm sure
all of you are thinking of these things as I speak,
how you found them,
and how you still find them, nudges, invitations.

Selected Homilies

Now look at this part of it. No stage of life is necessarily final.
You plan your life along certain lines, then something happens
to pull you down to the heart of something you were missing.
You feel a new kind of experience: Paul thought he'd be a great Pharisee, observant
and faithful to the Torah, and that all changed;
Peter set out as a fisherman, Isaiah was an aristocrat and courtier.
Those things were set aside.
Something mysterious happened to prompt a change.

Have you ever set aside your ordinary journey, your first love:
for me it was teaching English, being in a classroom.
I loved it. To this day I remember opening up the possibility
of conducting romance, of flirting, by conversation,
as they do it in *Pride and Prejudice*. Undergraduate fiction class.
And then there comes a nudge toward something different.
A phone call, a job at Milford, the spirituality center.
Hmmm. Has this been what I have been trying to do anyway,
expand the potential of people's basic experience of life and feeling.
This is accompanied by a kind of lift of the heart,
that place where you look for God. Jesus present right there.

And I certainly know among this congregation
how taking up something new creates a new sense of one's self:
passing up a business venture to become a teacher;
setting aside a few weeks of summer vacation or job or sports
to set out to Harlan, Kentucky.
You know when you are moved to try something.
It's more than skills assessment. It's a hunch, maybe even with reluctance.
And it leads you to something else,
maybe a year of volunteer work after college.
And then your life is kind of ruined, isn't it.
A new and deeper and mysterious purpose starts to claim you.

And further, and finally, notice this.
These stories of Paul, Isaiah, Peter, the men and women

Richard Bollman, SJ

who were called and invited and sent out in the early days,
these stories of spiritual purpose, when they break open,
we start to see that our prerequisites for this are not cleverness or talent,
but our weakness, our broken hearts and troubles, our vulnerable points.
We recognize our unclean lips, we start to feel the pain of our wrong choices,
we are amazed at how self-centered, and how sinful we can be.
And more amazing, Jesus steps right into that mess with us,
and says: "now you see who you are. How wonderful,
and how I love you in this honesty and this mixed mess you've made."
This is how our lives become ministry, something beyond careers.
Our own redemption is a source of good news and benefit for others.

So, when Peter stresses his sinfulness and inexperience,
Jesus doesn't deny it, doesn't try to make him feel better.
He takes it as true: and then works with it anyway.
"It's time for you to trust me," that's the word Jesus brings to us.
"Time to trust my love and grace, and to let your life expand.
Your youth or your pain or doubt are no obstacle for me.
From now on you will gather people,
you will touch the core of life itself.
You will understand your limits and sinful condition and not regret it
or look back with sadness.
And in everything that is in front of you now, your hand is in mine."

That's what the poem is about, the Rilke lines I quoted.
the one that begins: "God speaks to each of us as he makes us."

God speaks to each of us as he makes us,
then walks with us silently out of the night.

These are the words we dimly hear:

You, sent out beyond your recall,
go to the limits of your longing.
Embody me.

Flare up like a flame
and make big shadows I can move in.

Selected Homilies

Let everything happen to you: beauty and terror.
Just keep going. No feeling is final.
Don't let yourself lose me.

Nearby is the country they call life.
You will know it by its seriousness.

Give me your hand.

"Gott spricht zu jedem.../God speaks to each of us..." from RILKE'S BOOK OF HOURS: LOVE POEMS TO GOD by Rainer Maria Rilke, translated by Anita Barrows and Joanna Macy, translation copyright © 1996 by Anita Barrows and Joanna Macy. Used by permission of Riverhead, an imprint of Penguin Publishing Group, a division of Penguin Random House LLC. All rights reserved.

learning to follow

3rd Sunday, B
Jonah 3:1-2; Mark: 1:14-20

The word of the LORD came to Jonah a second time:
Set out for the great city of Nineveh, and announce to it the message that I will tell you. So Jonah set out for Nineveh, in accord with the word of the LORD. (Jonah 3:1-2)

Then they abandoned their nets and followed him. (Mark 1:18)

Richard Bollman, SJ

HOMILY

On Saturday this past week, I was with about two dozen people
who represented four parishes involved in a beginning,
something we feel is happening,
this community organization called, for now, UCAN.
United Churches Active in Neighborhoods.
Or maybe not active yet, but together wondering
whether we can be active in neighborhoods
working with one another, not separately.
Like Jonah, we ruminate these things, we make a cautious move.

Working together has advantages:
it cuts across racial lines, and across different church lines.
And it increases the number of people to tackle something,
whether that's an education project or visiting nursing homes
or getting publicity about neglected housing.

Lauren Renneker and ten committed parishioners
having been involved in the meetings and trainings
and slow start-up of this effort.
One other Catholic parish, St. Francis Seraph from Over-the-Rhine,
has a longer experience in this,
as do a number of African-American protestant churches,
and often their pastors show up, as they did yesterday.

Because yesterday's goal was to decide on a project.
To start planning to do something.
This put everybody outside of their comfort zone, moving toward action.
It's one thing for me to help plan a parish project,
but another thing to plan with a Black Episcopal priest
or a group of Baptist women from a parish at Findlay and Elm;
another thing, even, to meet the Franciscan parishioners
from Liberty and Vine, with their own special passion for ministry.
And yet, the people who planned the meeting yesterday
had a clean procedure, and the issues that concerned the different parishes

where people felt some commitment to work,
got narrowed down to urban housing,
with one very specific, very do-able job,
to bring a building up to code:
a senior citizen apartment in the West End.
At this point, UCAN, which has been a speculative conversation,
stepped into a new realm.
There was prayer and singing, and some anxiety
and some excitement.
Just four churches, invited to leave their nets behind,
to step out of the familiar boat,
and to follow what I think can be recognized
as a call, something moving from the Lord.

It reminded me of something I do believe,
but never like to face up to:
that when you say Yes to any kind of calling,
you may think you're going to change the city or the world,
but the main thing that changes is YOU.
Or, put another way, the work of faith is not
"doing good," but it is letting God do something,
and that means your fear, your private agenda,
can be set aside. In other words, you have to repent.

This is the point of our remembering the story of great callings.
It's not just that a fine thing happened
to John or James, or Jonah or Jesus.
It is a story about our common condition,
where the moment is now, and the approach of God is real,
and the word is: follow me, follow Jesus, follow the call.
And when we leave the boat to get involved,
when we leave the familiar and comfortable,
we step into the way of personally changing:
putting aside fear, competition, pet projects,
putting aside blaming and controlling others,
and venturing into a place where God has room to be with us
in the work of community.

Richard Bollman, SJ

I could have called this the work of justice,
but I don't like that word so much,
since it connotes courtrooms and playing fair,
legal or distributive justice: which is good,
but which is not exactly what the Bible means by justice.

The Bible's word for justice is Good News,
or Dominion of God: which is to say,
a world that works, a community that is safe and fruitful,
a harmony among neighborhoods, God's spirit guiding things,
people doing right by themselves and doing right by each other.
Laws matter, of course, but mainly
people have to meet and get the facts
and speak from their hearts.
Then it's not just doing for others,
but everybody figuring out how to do what they can,
willingly and respectfully, for one another.

I think of our parishioners Martha Stricker and Paul Knitter,
staying with the peace process in Salvador,
being part of the North American voice of concern,
part of the Church wanting to understand
and share what they can of compassion and insight.
The time is fulfilled, the dominion of God is ready,
and we need to listen, to repent and believe.

So, when you hear such a story as this one,
Jesus passing the fishermen at the lake,
or when you read about United Churches Acting in Neighborhoods,
or our youth group building houses in Appalachia,
or Martha and Paul in Salvador,
this is not just a lot of additional "stuff" in people's lives,
this is very basic life, according to the faith we all follow.
There we are, stepping out of our comfort zone, leaving those nets,
and venturing into the larger power of God's hopes for us.

Selected Homilies

Surely you've heard such a voice too.
When you were born, when you left home to go to kindergarten,
when you joined cross country or the debate team,
when you for the first time decided not to judge somebody different
but to understand them instead,
thousands of ways of leaving your nets
and going out closer to where God is inviting you.
Through all these decisions, up into marriage and your professions,
the yearnings inside us–
notice also the voice of one who guides you
into these places of risk and surrender.
When we realize, yes, we are being called,
this does not add a dreary weight to life,
but rather lifts the weight.
We're no longer so self-concerned and controlling,
so worried and fearful.
We're closer to the good news that is
the hidden stream of every life.

So, today, allow Jesus just to look at you,
and see through to what you really want to be and do.
You may have forgotten how truly fine a vision you have,
and how much God wants to accomplish in you
of healing, loving, giving life.
It is God who makes all things new.
It is we who must repent of
having to do it all ourselves!

Richard Bollman, SJ

trusting the one you know

21st Sunday, A
Matthew 16:13-20

He said to them,
"But who do you say that I am?"
Simon Peter said in reply,
"You are the Messiah, the Son of the living God." (Matthew 16:15-16)

HOMILY

I have a hard time finding my way with this Gospel, how it should be told.
It can come across as a kind of administrative or catechism lesson,
with wrong and right answers.

I've been helped to get closer to this moment looking into the place:
Caesarea Philippi. This is the only event in the New Testament
that occurs around that town, "in the region," says the story,
and that area is lush and different from the towns of Galilee,
north as it is, above the big lake, through a valley that holds
the first streams of the river Jordan.
There you are in the shadow of Mt. Hebron.
The mount itself once held a shrine for the god Pan,
and so for the Romans, it was a place of prayer and celebration,
music, dance, costumes, one would expect,
and ruins of the shrine and villas are still there.
Likely it was not a place Jesus went toward for the sake of teaching
but more for the change it brought, the cool water of the river,
the fertile valley itself, and this helps me to think of this story
not as a lesson or a quiz but a kind of conversation,
inching toward some new moment of mutual understanding,
Jesus and the disciples.

Think of this then as a real inquiry: "what do you hear from people,
what are they saying about me now, after these months
in the Galilee towns, the countryside, the healings and teaching."
We can sit in on this, a camping site, a late supper, stories remembered.

So let it be a question of importance for you this evening:
what DO you know of Jesus, what people tell you,
who he is, what he wants, how he matters.
Thinking back, he was once approached by followers of the Baptist,
and they ask him this same question: are you the one
or should we wait for another?
We remember Jesus saying to these seekers: Look around.
"The blind see, lepers are cleansed, the deaf hear, the dead are raised,
the poor have the Gospel preached to them." This is what people tell about.
And this is the Jesus we learn about in school, in the Sunday Gospels,
in a movie maybe, or a popular history of the era.
It is what we know: this attractive person who helps make people whole,
out of a powerful love, or mercy, wanting to enrich lives, transform them.

Were Jesus to ask me what I hear lately, I'd tell him about
the Habitat house opening yesterday. The Miller family,
mother and daughter, and their friends, and parish members from here
and all the communities of our coalition, celebrating a beautiful new home,
over there in Walnut Hills. Surrounded it was by
all those who worked and helped,
a group so diverse in worship tradition and color and youth and age.
Pastor Jerry Gray of Christ Emmanuel Fellowship
looked out on all of us and said in his prayer: "This is the Body of Christ.
This is what the Body of Christ looks like."
And I got that: it landed right in the center of this Gospel.
What do people say of me? Here you are gathering folks to build a house.

And I could tell about that Body of Christ here in this chapel, at this table,
in these great songs and prayers, because there is Christ among us,
I count on that, and I could say: this is what I hear, what I think I know.

Richard Bollman, SJ

But then comes something else. Even as we assimilate together
what we can say about our own learning and listening to the tradition,
there comes a second question in that cool valley, as the day ended.
He said, "and You, Richard, or Mary Ann or Debra or Jim."
(This is how the story goes.) "You, who do you say that I am?
Who have you come to know in knowing me?"

Peter's answer is not my answer much any more.
Christ/Messiah, Son of God, it's more part of my past, a theology course.
I think a person has to venture a little silence with this question,
and then a good bit of wondering, getting to your own experience and place.
And this question, I think, is the more important one for Jesus too,
for I think it comes from a desire to be known exactly now,
to be known from another human mind and heart: yours and mine.
Not with theological precision, but with something else, soul conviction,
something person to person.

Venture into that, I think: something of what you might feel as friendship,
or a kind of awestruck uncertainty. Or this respectful glance at the rabbi,
the good teacher, you feel close to, you stay with, cling to even,
for sanity each day. Friendship, I think, and practical experience, and well,
the beginnings of love. This is what might come up.
A friendship, a presence, that is maybe even open to doubt,
or to screwing up somewhere, able to stay steady with our own inconsistency.
Because the one close to us, opening up this question, is so very willing.

Where do you most meet this moment?
I remember meeting up with an old friend not many months before he died,
a man who valued a Gospel painting in his office, something from years ago;
it was of Jesus, and Peter and the disciples walking through the wheat field.
It mattered to him, but he didn't know why
until he was diagnosed with a serious un-treatable cancer.
This caused him to sit down differently, to take this in, to say what he could,
to take it all in and maybe find words, with his wife and his friends.
And then once sitting there just to himself, looking at the painting,

Selected Homilies

noticing for the first time that Jesus and Peter were a bit out in front,
in the foreground, and he saw how Jesus was touching Peter's arm.
Just that. A connection got made, then and forever, that said everything
about Jesus now, about knowing and feeling one another.

Is this you maybe? Underneath what we know from books
there is the theology of our inner senses, the almost actual feel
of a hand on our arm.

So it is that Jesus strictly charged the disciples not to go around
talking it up, telling everybody about the Christ.
Nothing would be really understood. Coming to love Jesus,
to relate to him, to know the presence even now, it's different for us all.

Pay attention to it these days. Maybe you know a place
where trees or a pond or a garden or the far edge of a playing field
give you a place to be yourself. And wonder about him.
How he wants to know you, and be in touch as you can let it happen.
The dear urgency and friendship in the question.

Let it come very close to you, your mind and soul.

Richard Bollman, SJ

5. THE PASCHAL STORY

A paschal story is our life itself, allowing for what dies, and how a new life comes from that radical change. That ancestral liberation from Egypt involved giving up a kind of security held in a rigid society of servitude, risking then the death of ease and safety on that long wilderness trek toward the Promise. Jesus lived this continuing story in his family traditions of prayer. And it led him to risk obedience to a new journey given by God, in which once again he named all the idolatry that holds us back. He professed what he came to see even though it demanded his life in return.

So Lent concerns this waking up to our deeper selves, with its bondage and uncertainties, our own good choices, bad choices, wherever we are on that journey.

giving up

1st Sunday of Lent, A
Genesis 2:7-9, 3:1-7; Romans 5:12-19; Matthew 4:1-11

Lent begins with the 2nd Creation story, not the seven days, but the making of the original human pair, the man, the woman. And it includes another aspect of the beginnings, how their eyes were opened to the differences in themselves between good choices and bad choices. Knowing this.

And then, Paul to the Romans explores the meaning of Jesus Christ as a new kind of human being, this second Adam, who knows himself, knows God, who also struggles to make the good choices. In the Gospel we find an account of Jesus sorting out the temptations we all deal with. It is a dialogue with the dark spirits, held up to us this first Sunday.

HOMILY

Let me bring up an example of this kind of experience Jesus had,
waking up to an interior struggle, getting a glimpse of inner choices.
It is a kind of humble example I realize, but it is real enough,
and connected specifically to our own time and place.
It comes from a friend of mine who openly confessed,
"I've become an addict: I realize I'm addicted to the news. It's bad for me."
(I did not toss this off as a joke. It's not the first time I've heard such a thing.)
She went on: "it's not about events, this fact or that, it's the commentaries.
I can't get enough: CNN, MSNBC, PBS, all the interpretations,
all the pundits and predictions. It just takes over."
And then she added the darker part of it, "saying I know I'm not really informed.
I'm not getting anything I need. It's like my brain is just taken over."

I told her some things I had been reading by the religion editor
of *The Washington Post*; her name is Diana Bass.
She writes how she feels that political commentators have colonized her soul.
This is in a column about Lent. Isn't it a time to "give up" stuff, she writes,
all that distracts you from life,
all that brings you down or gets in the way.
What are you giving up for Lent? "Consider giving up the media for Lent."
That's how she put it.

So with these examples in my mind, I pictured Jesus going off to the desert
but bringing along his smart phone, hanging on to what's happening,
what he ought to be afraid of, who's maybe going to win a new appointment,
or what member of Herod's court is about to be thrown out.
Keeping in touch about his own reputation, what people made of him at the river.
Indeed these voices might have been buzzing in his brain even without media.

What would it be to set this stuff aside, to see through it,
or at least to give up the steady sound of it, the scrolling headlines,

Richard Bollman, SJ

the talking or shouting matches, with the ball scores running underneath.
Instead of listening and watching,
take some time to read, or go on a hike, or do some gardening.

My friend said she wants to work out a plan to get
what she needs of daily events without commentary, without the hype.
What she wants to give up is the falsity: turning stones into bread,
to give up plunging off the electric tower into her biases and fears,
or adding up your power over people, who to blame, who to get the best of:
to give up even your fears, in favor of something else.
In favor of the word of God, trusting God alone, that bare hope.

Now let me come clean: if you know me, you know my attachments
are not social media, the evening news, not even *The New York Times*.
Alas, no, I escape my worries on movie screens, big and little screens,
not just once for the Oscar nominees, but two times or three times,
the world of images and dramatic music and great editing and story.
Needing to see it again: that scene at the table, was that where the little boy
came to see he could trust the drug dealer, is that what happened?
That smile at the end of the musical, what did it mean for the jazz pianist?
I pick this up. And I feel full. But am I hiding from some bigger truth
of my own growing up or falling in love or coming to the aid of my neighbor,
or standing up for what I believe in, or maybe just avoiding real people,
all the while sitting in the dark with strangers.

In all of this we have to ask, is there something tucked away
in all the news and phoning and entertainment, some hidden prayer
for what we truly desire, for the actual hopes we have,
a prayer that we might want to make actually to God
to God alone in the desert, naked and exposed, as Jesus seems to be
in today's story. That prayer: to blurt it out in the face of the devil.
"Here is what I believe, what I need, what I am invited to do. Here I am.
God come close to me, who you are, the words that come from your mouth
and the words that I want to say back to you!"

This is a prayer rising up from the plight of the addict,
as my friend brought it up in the first place:

Selected Homilies

the media as a place of addiction.
We all live in that place of temptation: we live in an addictive society,
as you know, when you talk to a friend by text messages
when she might be sitting across the hall in her own room,
or across the breakfast table.

"Addiction" is something that shows up whenever we notice
that our real life has gotten torn away from its moorings,
and we are unable to manage what it means really to live well.
And most important, when we admit the problem!
We admit the attachment, the craziness, the unreality.
Then we are moving toward the light.
Then, something can happen. Then you begin to see
that the Gospel is not far from the wisdom of the 12 Steps.
You've heard of these, I'm sure. The path to recovery.
Well here's what the 2nd step says:
"We come to believe . . . that a power greater than ourselves . . .
can restore us to sanity."

The first step is what I described moments ago, that we fess up,
something is not working for me, for us.
And then, listen to this. In the midst of the struggle,
"we come to believe. . . ." (that slow dawning!)
"that a power greater than ourselves . . ." (we are not in charge now!)
"can restore us to sanity."

That's the story of the Gospel today. It's a "second step" story.
It is happening within Jesus: coming to that kind of faith.
Coming to that kind of desire for sanity. For a real life, for the holy,
for the ordinary human.

And what is this sanity? I think of Walter Burkhardt's definition of contemplation:
sanity is "a long, loving look at the real."
It is loving the truth, trusting the real world of facts, what is actual in the moment,
the gaze of your own heart, your eyes and ears. Sanity.
It is what we sometimes call "the mind of Christ," the word of God,

Richard Bollman, SJ

Wanting it: and coming to believe Christ is there for you.
Not in your own made up stuff, your own wishes to change,
but in the power of one who wants to join you in the struggle.

So here is the first Week of Lent. Unfolded in a story,
and felt in our own lives through our attachments and addictions.
This then is the fasting we are called to, the prayer, the service
we are invited to choose. Admitting these attachments,
seeing through the stones and the risks and the lies,
and coming to faith in one who is powerful with us already.
And that's where our hope for freedom emerges.

Not our own power, but the higher power that is the Word given to us
in the darkness and the desert.

finding yourself

1st Sunday of Lent, A
Romans 5:12-19; Matthew 4:1-11

Jesus was led by the Spirit into the desert . . . (Matthew 4:1)

HOMILY

Going to the desert is an old way of finding yourself,
a testing of the inner spirit, like a vision quest.
You are looking for the essentials that will guide your life.

Why the desert?
Part of it is learning to negotiate danger.
Part of it is learning our essential solitude.
One key essential is the absence of clear roads:
you have to find your way by a new learning of what to notice.
Maybe you meet angels to help, maybe the devil.
You have to learn which is which.

Everyday life is a desert quest.
Of course you know your way to work or school, that's easy.
But you may go to a school where you don't yet know
who your friends are, what attitude you want to try out,
or whether you can talk to anybody about what's on your mind.
Just that–the testing of teenagers: danger in the air,
a lot to sort out about your friends, about your future,
maybe drugs or guns not far from where you have to go,
maybe the shock of a suicide in the neighborhood or a divorce next-door.

We're tested. As a Church, obviously, we're tested:
How do we sort out our feelings about faulty leadership,
what is the grief we carry for people who have been abused, or misled.
What is it to listen to our own voices as lay people and lay ministers.
Meanwhile we crowd our schedules, at home and parish,
with meetings, responsibilities, wanting to get your way,
efforts to please people, you know what it's like.

Jesus, we must remember,
is not a superior being who easily tells the devil where to get off.
Jesus is a human being tempted by his hunger,
tested by his need to succeed,
torn between grandiosity and humility.
His rejection of Satan is a real sifting of soul. He is brother to us.
What seems to me the heart of Jesus' search
is his growing trust in the word of God.

Richard Bollman, SJ

Notice how he grounds himself by remembering who God is.
It's not just that he quotes the Bible at the devil.
The devil quotes the Bible back at him.
But the devil's use of scripture is like a fundamentalist approach.
The devil takes every word literally:
and therefore Jesus should jump and expect angels to rescue him.
But Jesus has appropriated the heart of the Bible
which is the deep truth that God is trustworthy,
and God wants to be in relationship with us in the dangers.
Maybe you are finding this too:
God is more than a rescue on a dangerous journey,
God leads the journey and is present in it all the time.
That's what life constantly teaches us, when we listen:
and the Bible helps us to find that voice, that presence.

We open the scripture not just to read, but to listen.
And out of that experience, even just listening on Sundays,
we are drawn gradually into relationship, into knowing one another.

Listening to God is awkward at first
because we expect a lot of information maybe:
we go to God with questions and want answers,
or we expect to be accused, or blamed–that can get in the way.
That's like trying to turn stones into bread.
Relationship is simpler than that.

The word that proceeds from the mouth of God is first of all our name:
Carol, Dan, Anna, Kristy, Joe. That's what we dare to expect.
This is direction in the wilderness, all through scripture:
Moses, Moses; Hail Mary; Saul, Saul.
The risky moment in our everyday desert then,
is when you pause to be still and listen awhile to your heart beat, breathing,
and your name in the center of that still place.

Maybe all you can do, briefly before you get out of the car
is to say: here we go. God, recognize me.

Selected Homilies

We like to say, God help me, but that can be too casual almost,
and it doesn't say much about yourself.
But as you let your name be known, as you want to be recognized,
you can explore your moment a little, giving it over:
"I feel nervous today, or lost, or excited, or wondering."
It's a whole new world, giving yourself to God like this.
You know you are living by something more than bread.

So that's what I recommend to your journey,
some daily practice of giving yourself over: listening for your name,
offering what you can of your own living spirit.
That's why we fast during Lent,
whether we fast from food or drink or from shopping or surfing the web.
We have to learn our real hungers and to trust God in the risky places.

I read about a young man in a long process of recovery from cancer.
He said his greatest temptation was to turn away from faith
and to put on religion, to ask God to free him from the test,
to pray for a miracle.
As he resisted that temptation, his usual strengths were torn away
and he began to trust God without demanding anything from God,
without needing anything to change.
And then he found a new strength, unknown energies, to keep heart
and to value the gift of life just as it is.
"We are made this way," he said. "We can also be ill!"

We are all together in this kind of wonderful moment,
as Church, as friends, as individuals,
getting used to a God who is more compelling and deeper
than the God of religion, a petition for rescue.
When like Jesus we are shaken with real need,
when we sense the suffering of the poor, the embattled stranger,
we can find a way to our own heart too, in solidarity, not cut off,
and we enter this intensely mysterious, sorrowing, and beautiful life;
and we say Amen, let's worship and give thanks for who we are.
Little by little, in this way, we come safely through the test.

Richard Bollman, SJ

learning to see

4th Sunday of Lent, A
John 9

The Gospels midway in Lent tell of encounters with Jesus that led to a turning point, a conversion in a person's life. Like this blind man, touched and healed, but not fully new until he comes to understand his own internal differences, his unexpected role in the community, and the direct influence of Christ in this and in his future involvement with faith and action. We are this person; it is not a past even, but a present account of how God works in us. Be sure to read the whole story, John chapter 9.

HOMILY

Here we have the account of a man who suddenly is able to see,
for the first time in his life. This is something that happens in a total way,
not just being able to use his eyes. Well beyond that pleasure,
there comes new light to his whole situation.
It is a growth in human understanding, and growth in faith too.
It doesn't happen all at once, but shows a kind of search.
He was learning a new life. And he couldn't explain it adequately.
It was hard to get people to pay attention, to be really interested.

So he finds his neighbors interested in what happened, but
they reduce it to questions of How? When? Who?
and as he answers such questions, he sees that not much is understood.
His own experience of himself is never really explored.
What's it like to see? To be you? What can you tell us of your experience?

Selected Homilies

Even his parents back away. They are concerned with the public issue.
They might be expelled from the synagogue if this story gets out.
"Why put yourself through this, why endanger us?"

And then when it all comes to the attention of church authorities,
he is not able to have his own story, to declare his own life. It's not wanted.
They say they are deeply interested in the man's reality
but they could not go to the level of life where he really was living.
That is a deeper realm of encounter with God, of change, of altered priorities.
Certain kinds of changes within a woman or man just can't be explained
through a juridical Q and A. But you can't erase them, or go back.
Your daughter returns from a year's work as a volunteer in Guatemala
and you don't know what to think, how to relate to her;
you have to move beyond questions and explanations
into personal experience. Body and soul. Who is she now?

It reminds me of what is happening in the African-America community,
where the story of Civil Rights has changed into "Black Lives Matter,"
which can't be understood by linguistic analysis or reasoned arguments.
No, this is not like saying "White Lives Matter."
This is not countered by exploring just who gets shot at, who goes to jail.
What is called for is an in-depth appreciation of life circumstances
felt from within, from within families, within bodies and souls,
within feelings and love and the long stories, true history,
commitments too, reaching down to a place where human beings
finally might meet, but it takes a while, it requires vulnerable listening
and new, willing attention among everybody.
I think it's this kind of thing that is happening
among the Parkland high school students, a deep shift about life,
about teenagers glossed over by the adult world,
and what it's like, just going to school.
What real change would feel like.

So yes, you can analyze why do people get shot at,
you try to reason your way through this gap in understanding
among human communities,
but our Gospel story today suggests that you need to proceed

Richard Bollman, SJ

to the level of spiritual intuition, human experience and suffering,
and then you begin to grasp how events have something to say
about the work of God among us. That's what we might come to know.
"Why was he born blind?" Not that we can convict him or his family
but so that the works of God might be revealed.
God at work. So God looks to where we are open to change,
willing to see things new. There God is at work.

Just recently I picked up this book I finished reading:
It's not long; it's called *Building a Bridge*. A bridge between people
where they take the time to grasp difference,
where they can walk in both directions, and tell their story and be understood.
That's what was lacking for the man born blind: there was no bridge
of relationship: no place for respectful hearing, compassion, sensitivity
with his neighbors, his parents, the religious authorities.
The subtitle of this book, by James Martin, is
"How the Catholic Church and the LGBT Community
can enter into a relationship of respect, compassion, and sensitivity."
It came out over a year ago, but I waited for the paperback,
which turns out to be a bit enlarged and clarified.

But the main story is this: gay men and women need to be seen,
by the actual church in its leaders. And church leaders in turn
need to be seen and understood, appreciated, by the gay community.
Respect, Compassion, Sensitivity. This is needed on both sides.
It will not happen by just seeing from afar,
looking at a picture of cardinals lined up in St. Peter's basilica,
or imagining a group of guys going to a gay bar in some local neighborhood.
This is not a time for seeing just with your eyes and forming judgments.
Relationship happens when stories are explored and listened to
and wondered about in the whole realm of life,
our bodies and souls, commitments, home and families. In all faith,
where is the work of God being revealed?
With respect, sensitivity, compassion.

So there it is, what I propose we take from the Gospel:
the man born blind was not all-at-once engaged with Christ as Christ is,

Selected Homilies

or even with himself as he was becoming.
It all happened slowly,
to manifest the works of God as they can come to light,
day by day, going through how you are met and what comes alive
as you bump into one another,
as you hear stories from family life and schooling,
early jobs and creative hopes,
as you find Christ in the life you are given,
Christ who is always looking for you.

Looking to be with you: not only black or gay, or a high school teen.
A bishop or a country pastor, a teacher or athlete.
Christ who knows what it is like to really be who you are.
As yourselves. Isn't it true that each Sunday, really,
you are a little different from last Sunday,
the Gospel always expanding you,
this hymn or friendship, always reshaping you just a little,
and opening up for you to find yourself and your priorities
more effectively: learning how to respect people,
and to stand with them, to give of your time and prayer together,
all of this, something going on
that we gradually can recognize as the work of God.
Happening because we have followed a call to come together.
Here, on this bridge.

Not to be blind to the work of God
hidden in human lives of all kinds.
Not to be blind. But to see.

The Lenten Gospels walk us along to the deep turning point of death, Christ with us there, in the unanswerable. When I visit a grave side, I think of things I want to tell that person underground, and I think maybe I should pray for them, and then I wonder where are they now, and before long the questions pour out,

Richard Bollman, SJ

don't they! The grave side is a place where we don't know much. Except for the silence under that stone. And the new silence in our own life.

So we let the Gospel come to mind, just the broad telling of it, how Christ too at a graveside would feel the silence. The memories. It is said that Jesus wept for his friend who died. I think it's allowed that he would weep for our own brother or sister, our child, our mother, for he knew them, tenderly, better than we knew them. He knows us too at the grave, and is willing to enter our own silence, our tears, letting his own tears come. At the edge of what we can ever know, at the margins, he stands with us.

Are we being called, right now in our daily lives, toward a trust and a freedom that begins to alter everything? This edge of the season of wonder: some kind of actual faith, a trust reaching across boundaries, the great thawing of what is frozen. "Get up, he is calling you."

the raising of Lazarus, 1

5th Sunday of Lent, A
John 11:1-45

When Jesus arrived, he found that Lazarus had already been in the tomb for four days. When Martha heard that Jesus was coming, she went to meet him; but Mary sat at home. Martha said to Jesus, "Lord, if you had been here, my brother would not have died. [But] even now I know that whatever you ask of God, God will give you." (John 11:17, 20-22)

HOMILY

The story tells us about people who are coming to believe.
They haven't arrived yet, but they are coming, like Martha, coming to faith.
Like her neighbors and friends, they are beginning to believe.

That feels right to me. The story makes me ponder my own faith,
its quality and maturity.
What do I make of the revelation of Jesus in this story?
it is such a bridge to cross.

Other miracles of Jesus are easier to tolerate:
I believe in healing, for example,
that the laying on of hands, the energetic encounter of love,
a gift of insight into where people are hurting--
all these things can work.
So, I can get close to Jesus as a faith healer,
or Jesus as prophet, Jesus as reformer of religion,
the one who forgives, who reconciles hearts;
Jesus as friend and as promise of a life after death.

Life after death: even that is comprehensible in some way,
not fully known of course,
but there is "life after death" witness now!
People have been on that brink and come back to tell about it.
I believe in the resurrection.
But life 4 days later after burial, that's unnerving.

But I think this story has to be here.
We have to let it work.
In it we see ourselves, just on the brink of faith.

You see, like us, everybody in the story
knew of Jesus' reputation as a healer.
They were quite okay with that.
They knew of him as one who had opened the eyes of the blind.
They knew he forgave sin, and that he was calling for
some kind of new way of life and relationship
that made him unpopular
with the current religious authorities.

Richard Bollman, SJ

They knew, in other words, the Jesus that we like best.
They believed that, had Jesus been there,
Lazarus would have gotten well.
Jesus himself seems to acknowledge this.
Yes, if I had been there, he'd have gotten well,
and I'm glad I wasn't there: for YOUR sake. For OUR sake.

Why "for our sake?" Because here he has something else to show.
And that is not his power. No, this is not a story about
Jesus' special powers.
It is about his faith in God.
And that's what we need to realize.
Jesus had faith in God. This is what he is about.

It is the woman Martha who utters the word
that opens up the meaning of this story.
She says to him: "I know that
whatever you ask of God, God will give you."
She is the true interpreter of this story; she gets the point.

So this is a story about Jesus and the God he believes in,
the God he knows very intimately, and trusts beyond anything.
The God he daringly recommends even to us. NOW.
And in the same moment we meet Jesus as very much a human being.
Jesus weeps for our sorrow
because he is human, emotional, involved in our situation.
He is wrenched by losses, saddened by wasted opportunity,
frustrated by disfunctional systems: family, parish, city, church.
He cries out for hurricane victims, and political prisoners:
for this human wretchedness.
He takes it personally.

It's almost as if the Teacher wants us to know first
that even he cannot change things all the time.
Even he is not at our beck and call for miracles.
But he feels life with us.

Selected Homilies

This is essential to the Jesus in this story.
And in that vulnerable place, his faith is immensely strong.

He says: Take me to the place where the stone is rolled over death.
Take me to the place where the abyss opens up,
where your fear and loss and anger
shake you so thoroughly you cannot even reason,
you lose your coping skills,
where you say: don't even ask to expose this room of death,
because every ounce of opportunity, justice, beauty,
has been snuffed out.

Where is that, the doorway to the impossible?
Here in this impossible place, the Teacher says, Jesus says,
let us join in faith together.
EVEN SO, the glory of God can shine here.
Whether you live with chronic pain or disability
or the erosion of spirit that comes from abuse,
joblessness, failure.
Even so, the Glory of God shines here, prayer comes to mean something.
Here where there is nothing left, there is this faith,
the faith that moved Jesus,
that supported him in failure,
in fear, in giving up his life.
Faith that does not shrink from the fact of death,
from the stench and decay of what we face as humans.
All that is real.
Take away the stone: let there be no doubt.

The Teacher is here, with a great prayer:
God, I know that you hear me! I know that you hear me.
That is the faith of Jesus.
That is his prayer.
And then a shout into the darkness,
Lazarus come out.

Richard Bollman, SJ

He relies on that love of God which keeps coming
not from his own power but from his trust,
when there isn't any reason in the world for it to happen.

Come out, he says. Here is where faith begins.

the raising of Lazarus, 2

5th Sunday of Lent, A
Romans 8:8-11

If the Spirit of the one who raised Jesus from the dead dwells in you, the one who raised Christ from the dead will give life to your mortal bodies also, through his Spirit that dwells in you. (Romans 8:11)

HOMILY

Yesterday I attended a funeral at a Missionary Baptist Church in Norwood.
The deceased was the younger sister of our former cook
at the Jesuit community ten years ago or so.
Carolyn would often bring her sister to the kitchen
between Cathy's schooling and the end of Carolyn's work day.
Cathy was born with Down Syndrome, and was easy to have around,
and Carolyn cared for her with all her heart, after her retirement
and up to her a death last week. It was not an easy loss for her, not at all.
But the funeral was a great lift.

There was applause for Cathy, the girl who died,
applause for her and for Christ raising her up now,
applause for the family and all of us there, great Amens
of presence and praise. There were tears and a kind of wailing.
The scriptures overflowed about new life,
Jesus the resurrection and the life,
all of this read with conviction by the pastor while the coffin was closed.
Then came great hymns, and the remarks of friends,
adding to the picture of a loved woman now with God,
as if she were indeed called forth from her earthly life now.
It was like the heavenly assembly took shape around us.
"Cathy, come out!"

Obviously, it reminded me of the family funeral in this Gospel story,
from Norwood then, to Bethany:
the tears and the wailing and the lifting up of hands,
the dear sense that the sisters had of Jesus who loved their brother,
all that love awakened again when Jesus arrived with his own tears,
and his own direct message to the sisters that life is still with us,
a new life we didn't expect, ready to come forth now.
And Martha was able to affirm that: she came to know and feel
what was no longer hidden. Christ Messiah, Son of God.
She could say it. It saved her.

That's the heart of this story: Jesus may at first seem absent,
but he is revealed in a great love that comes alive to claim us.
It is a personal love, tears from Jesus, from God, in friendship.
And it rises up in the feeling and faith of those who mourn,
who assemble together, who remove the heavy stone of death itself.

You know about this: you know it from your own family stories,
and from our bereavement ministry here, our shared losses.
and the assembling together:
and how a great presence comes in the assembly,
the resurrection lifting us up. Jesus calling us out.
Love is what stabilizes and affirms life, even at the brink of death.

Richard Bollman, SJ

This is not merely a theological realization,
but rather in something you can feel and be part of, something to touch,
with the preachers and singers and the weeping family,
something hidden within the human experience.

Here is another example of that love, and the hidden life within it.
I think of Helen Prejean's story of her work with condemned prisoners,
how intent she has been to be present at the moment of their death
and to make her love for them something they can know and trust.
It's like suddenly something which is very dark and painful and confusing,
becomes something a dying man can face, and even accept.
Love happens in the execution chamber,
or wherever we are distraught and afraid of dying.
And it reveals something powerful that is bigger than dying.
Take the stone away. Look upon this without fear.

There it is, the hidden presence of grace in our stories.
I remember my father's last days in the hospital,
through a procedure that irritated him greatly, a nasal tube designed
to relieve a bowel obstruction, and he was hard to be with,
so complaining that he had to be tied to the bed side
lest he again tear out the tube.
I could barely watch this or listen to his demands that we take him home.
It was like every tension of family life was being relived:
my sister and brother were gone for the day,
and finally, I fled.

Hours later, the nurse called me that the obstruction had passed.
And that he had been very comfortable. And then he rolled over
as she massaged him for bedtime, and just died. He had died with her.
He was not alone, I thought.

I said to the nurse, don't move him yet.
I drove to the hospital just to look upon him finally,
where the stone had been rolled away, and he was deeply himself,
dignified again, and present.

Selected Homilies

It was as if God had been laboring in him, toward this great peace,
and I see now that God had been laboring in my fears,
toward this reconciliation. Untie him, and let him go.

This is how it is with the resurrection and the life.
If only you had been here! we might say: The Christ of our desires.
But this is exactly where he is, where he resolutely stands with us.
This is where he belongs. At the edge, where we can't see very well.

Get up, he is asking for you.
The one who is coming into this world.
Take away the stone.

the raising of Lazarus, 3

5th Sunday of Lent, A

The hand of the LORD came upon me, and he led me out in the spirit of the LORD and set me in the center of the broad valley. It was filled with bones. He made me walk among them in every direction. So many lay on the surface of the valley! How dry they were! He asked me: Son of man, can these bones come back to life? "Lord GOD," I answered, "you alone know that." (Ezekiel 37:1-3)

HOMILY

About a week ago I listened to an African-American man
tell a story from his teen-age years.

Richard Bollman, SJ

This was a moment in a dialogue of black and white people
remembering racial encounters that have shaped their lives.
This man's story had to do with abuse, spitting and insults,
in detail that I don't want to repeat.
It took place because he was bright, and was among the first
to be bussed to a neighborhood school
when integration became the law of the land some forty years ago.

Listening to his story as a white man made me sorrowful and angry.
I felt the abuse had happened somehow in the name of all white people.
My heart was heavy and I wanted to apologize.

I feel a similar heaviness as a Catholic priest these days
in the wake of so many stories of young people,
now grown older, but still scarred by the abuse inflicted
by Catholic priests.
Even worse than the racial outrages, these events violated trust,
and sent the victim into a darkness of doubt, secrecy, and shared guilt.
And it is no surprise that a little of this news
angers anyone who cares about the Church,
and confirms the anger of people who have long since stopped caring.
Because sexual violations are the very thing
the Catholic church is seen to be uptight about through the years:
the violations of contraception even in a fruitful marriage,
the exclusion of a second marriage
without reference to circumstances or needs,
the abiding neglect of women's talent and calling and point of view,
the deaf ear turned to the experience of our gay sisters and brothers.

This heightens the hypocrisy of hidden sexual abuse,
and it's certainly easy to get caught in the quicksand of it,
both the painful acts and the frenzy of the media investigation,
and the years of broken lives and broken promises.
It's hard to bear.

I think of Ezekiel's question: can these bones live?
Ezekiel was a young Jew who survived the destruction of Jerusalem

somewhere six centuries before Christ,
and was deported with many of his Jewish countrymen
to Babylon. He was a refugee,
his religion and his culture was shattered.
Evidently he had a habit of praying in a valley near the city,
an old battlefield where the dead were so numerous
they had not been collected and buried over many years.
Like the killing fields of Laos and Cambodia, or the playgrounds of Kosovo.

He looked upon all this
and it called to mind his own people and his own life.
Can these bones live?
Only you know, God, only you know.

The question is very real for me, and for all of us I think,
in our Church today. And in our city too.
No one who stands for authority, government, the juridical system,
or the institutional church, gathers much credibility
on the streets of Cincinnati these days.
And we are all hurt by this. We can't stand aloof from it,
and just somebody else's problem.
What we feel as a church in the wake of sexual abuses
we ought also to be feeling
in the grip of long years of racial inequities, violence, and exclusion.
It hurts us all, because we really need one another
to make a social system, our own society, thrive.
We need each other's promises, and follow-through,
each other's honesty, respect,
we need laws that guide, and codes of ethics that make sense,
we need the wise ways of our grandparents,
we need the talent and voices of everybody.
Because we need social systems:
we need the Church, and a credible leadership of faithful disciples;
we need families,
in the same way we need a city to live in,
and a government to make it work.

Richard Bollman, SJ

Can these bones live?
The answer to this question, in light of our own faith,
is not another promise, not a strategy.
The answer is the person of Jesus.
In this woundedness and this death, Jesus weeps
because he has loved his brothers and sisters, and
he knows our homes and visits our table.

Those who associate with him, who eat his body and drink his cup,
are offered a way of life and relationship that is whole, and sacred,
that is the Spirit of Christ living in us.
That breath of spirit: the first thing it does
is to inspire forgiveness, which cuts through our own sinfulness,
which makes it possible to live more than just the life of the flesh,
the life of mortality and weakness.
It makes it possible to live a life restored filled up by God
from day to day, restored and forgiven and healed.
Not once and for all, but week by week.
Although "our bodies are subject to death,
our spirits are alive because of God's righteousness,"
because God has compassion upon all God has made,
and makes these bones to live again.

I came this weekend from a meeting of Jesuit superiors in Chicago,
a regular meeting we have twice a year,
but at this one there was much sharing of our hearts and minds
about the events of Boston and Florida,
the capacity of ourselves as church leaders to be defensive and embarrassed,
and the rights of the victims to be redressed.
We reviewed our own policies on sexual abuse,
just as the local diocese is reviewing its own procedures,
and the dominant theme is how to care for the ones who are wronged.

The irony of it is that the more the process is handled by the legal system
the harder it is for the perpetrator and the victim
to ever meet, to ever ask or give an apology,
to ever begin the long road of forgiveness.

But that is what heals, because these crimes arose out of trusted relationship,
they were not anonymous rape.
The damage is the death of spirit,
where a lawsuit and legal channels, no matter how lucrative,
turn out to be very limited where the core of life is hurt.

It is like the ashes of ground zero in New York, the bones still being found.
No amount of revenge or counter destruction
can actually penetrate this darkness.
And yet Jesus steps up to that awful place of stench and tears.
There is a gratitude in him.
Because now that death has done its worst,
his disciples, he hopes, will come to trust what God alone can accomplish.
"Roll away the stone," he says.
And even though there isn't a reason in the world
for it to make a difference,
he shouts into the darkness:
"Lazarus come out." Come out now. Come into the light.

And so it happens.
Unbind us holy Lord.
Unbind our racism and our sexual wounds,
our centuries of not caring. And set us free.

The days of Holy Thursday, and then Good Friday, ease a person into a quiet spirit, an open day, the decoration of churches, travel to your home town, the memory of friends who have helped you meet both the struggle and the hope of living. Signs of spring. And yet another journey to a grave side. And the tremors of an earthquake.

the world is not the way it has to be

Easter Vigil Mass and Sacraments
Matthew 28:1-10

After the sabbath, as the first day of the week was dawning, Mary Magdalene and the other Mary came to see the tomb. And behold, there was a great earthquake; for an angel of the Lord descended from heaven, approached, rolled back the stone, and sat upon it. (Matthew 28:1-2)

HOMILY

This is a story about God's doings.
You can tell that by the earthquake,
by the angel with the appearance of lightning.
We have to tell these stories, about God's power, that it is real.
We remember them on this solemn night:
a wind crosses the sea, and a path of dry land is opened up;
the ground shakes, an angel descends, and a stone is rolled away.
God is at work, and we can't express it any other way.
The story stretches our comprehension to a point of truth
beyond science, beyond the daily news.

The story contains an announcement to help us grasp its meaning.
It is given to women this time,
just as at the birth of Jesus it was given to shepherds–
people who are not part of the political or the temple establishment.
"Don't be afraid," the women are told; "Christ is raised.
He is raised and is already on his way to Galilee.
Go and tell the brothers and sisters who stayed at home,
they can expect to meet him."

Selected Homilies

This is what comes in the lightning and the fallen stone,
God doing something, raising Jesus out of the dark tomb,
acting in Jesus forever across space and time,
across the early morning fields and streets,
and even for us who sit here this night.
We hear that the women went to tell this story,
full of fear and yet overjoyed. Fear and Joy.
Not the old fearful anxiety and danger,
but a sense of amazement and expectation that now something new
can happen to us, after our deepest disappointment.
Something new can happen.
Like in the lives of the young people being baptized tonight,
sharing a sense of expectation, apprehension maybe,
but trusting this new thing that is happening.

These old stories of God doing something:
they are important because they awaken hope,
inspire reverence for new chances; they bring joy.

Rabbi Michael Lerner, an American Jew, reminds us that
telling the old stories is not just to talk about "the good old days."
He looks back on the story of Exodus, which we heard tonight.
The same God that made liberation possible then,
is making it possible for the world to be transformed and liberated even now,
from every kind of oppression. That power is still true.
This is revolutionary, the rabbi says: "The world is not the way it has to be."

I take heart from his words, hearing a Jew speak directly about this,
the spiritual transformation his own people need to hope for.
And this resides in the power of God acting, not in revenge or violence.
"The Occupation of Palestinian territory," he says,
"does not increase peace or security.
Uprooting land, bulldozing homes, this is how far we've fallen."
Rabbi Lerner is not influential on foreign policy. Here is a marginal voice,
but like the shepherds, the poor, the women of the gospel,
he has a cry of good news,
he points to God's power to change things.

Richard Bollman, SJ

I hear the same glimmers of new vitality in the voices
of the lay Church these days, Catholic journalists,
speaking freely about the need for new openness among the hierarchy,
an end to secrecy as a policy to save face.
Partly the energy rises up out of justified anger
at some bishops' face-saving negligence, and the recklessness
of too many priests' behavior. But this voice in the Church
is also saying "the Church is not the way it has to be."
What gives rise to this felt conviction?

I think it comes from faith, actual faith, in the truth of the New Testament,
stories of equal discipleship, of a new kind of community
of Spiritual gifts: prophecy, healing, leadership,
abundantly poured out through the spirit-filled Church.
These are the stories we will hear all through the Easter season,
and we've been taught that they hold a promise for all time.
This cry of good news, God's power to change things,
doesn't it inspire expectation, wonder, and the possibility of life!
As we let it become true, things change!

This is where we have to live our Easter, and begin
to send out from our own hearts
the felt possibility that the world is not the way it has to be;
the church is not the way it has to be; our city too,
not the way it has to be.
The stone is rolled away, and we find a new Christ
going before us, sending us out, and living in us too.

Suppose we believed this story, let its power work?
I know it's hard, because the tone of the daily news,
the rigid complaints about the city council on the one hand,
or the boycott on the other,
even the casual thought that we might combat terrorism with
strategic nuclear responses,
all this rigid system of death is designed to convince us
that nothing really ever changes, or can change.
But as a matter of fact WE can change.
There is wisdom enough

Selected Homilies

in the most ordinary person here tonight.
You know what makes life work, what makes it blessed,
you have a desire and a capability for the generous graciousness
that begins to affect for the better a family,
a household, a classroom or neighborhood.
We don't have to just march along drugged by what
the papers tell us to do and to believe.

Can we make a pledge: I ask you.
A pledge to live as if the resurrection of Jesus were upon us.
Our anxiety then would become an expectation that life shall come,
life will not be swallowed up. We have all come through the water.

So we make an Easter pledge:
a pledge first to admit our pain, not to hide behind old routines and games,
and not to blame each other for what we bear.
A pledge to respect ourselves and our community,
to affirm and encourage and to give up criticism.
A pledge to communicate our excitement, our feelings, our stories,
and to listen to what others value and want to say.
A pledge to apologize when we have hurt others,
and to forgive, seven times seventy, and not to hold grudges.
A pledge to honor life, and all living things around us, the living planet.

What might we become, with these simple choices?
And could such hopes begin to surround our city neighborhoods
and call us to stand with those who are treated unfairly,
and to believe every sign of grace,
whether it's a desire in a teenager for baptism,
or an overture from Saudi Arabia for peace in the middle east.

TIME magazine asks on its cover
Can the Catholic Church Save Itself?
Probably not.
It is God who saves. But it is God's community in Christ
who tell their story: the believers, the shepherds, the women—
who become the Church, the renewing Body of Christ, that saves.

Richard Bollman, SJ

I'm not praising its great holiness or political power.
That is not what I find to be hopeful in our Church.
It is rather the good sense of ordinary people
who trust God's goodness at the heart of things,
who find the law written on their hearts, learned in their woundedness.
This is what consoles me.
And it is happening now.

Rabbi Michael Lerner writes for www.tikkun.org. I am grateful for his permission to quote from his thoughtful writing.

toward Emmaus

3rd Sunday of Easter, A
Luke 24:13-35

Take time at this point to read again the Gospel story about the road to Emmaus. This is where Easter emerges as a story of our important friendships in faith, in sorrow, regret, and an entry into something new. It is our story in any era, particularly these years of challenge and change.

HOMILY

I've been troubled this Easter: worries, angers, regrets. At a low level,
I get messed up with the daily news, try to back off from that;
don't listen, it offers nothing, it riles you up.

Selected Homilies

But more painful are some illnesses and hard time with friends,
and in most instances they live far away from a visit or a reunion.
You know how even when a person is struggling it means a lot
to have time to sit with them. The Emmaus story gives me
something to mull over then. It helps me
get a feel for what life is like when you're on the way,
when you need distance and somebody with whom to talk things through.

I think of this couple then on their way out of town.
They deal with their own profound disappointments: "We had hoped."
I give credit to Cleopas and his friend, finding what they need so quickly.
I don't mean Jesus, I mean that they could actually get going somewhere.
They found each other in the suffering of their community.
Going deep, you might say. Sharing what they go through.

I think it must have been more than just the arrest of Jesus.
Think of their disbelief that close friends could not rescue him,
anger at how the Romans got involved, and shame that one's own leadership
simply got rid of him. It must have felt so personal.
Cleopas and the other one. Some think it would be his wife.
I have to imagine there were times between talk
when they just made their way not talking.
Something about a long walk can deepen what you find in yourself.
I would think they might finally explore a few hidden feelings,
how maybe they were themselves feeling ashamed they did so little,
knew Jesus so marginally,
expected too much of the wrong thing from him.
Why did he not reorganize the church, throw out the wasteful Vatican offices.
Or one might just blurt it out, "what use is there in being kind?
If things turned out this way, where your leader
resists violence and revenge, what hope is there for a new world?"
They might have surfaced such resentments.

I would expect between them, their own sorrow might have deepened
to include finally their own half-hearted faith.
You find your own sorrow coming up when you walk along,
and you might wish you were a more powerful woman or man,

Richard Bollman, SJ

able to manage and reform your own life anyway,
if not the church or city hall.

So a walk to Emmaus, I think it would be a time to explore your moment:
the regrets, wondering if we have loved well,
or if our faith isn't very half-hearted.
Seeing our limits, avoiding what we are afraid of.

I don't know how to put it. Often when I get close to my own real soul
I sort of inch along, just venture a little into the dark. Talk around things.
Not long ago I drove with a friend to Amish country, largely for her
to pick out a new chair: but she herself is negotiating more,
a great change in her life, able to speak of it more and more willingly,
but sitting with her in a grocery store café getting quiet
I could only think to say: what beautiful country around here,

I added "I'm just not up to feeling your distress, not just yet,
I tend to deal with things like this by denying. Holding it back and away."
She understood. Well I think she understood.
That might have happened on the road to Emmaus, even when
Jesus began to walk along too, and when he solicited their story.

So this is what Easter has been: several roads, several little towns.
And one great gift, even as I feel my own stuff time and again,
one great gift there is, in the way people are so very patient with me,
and giving me the gift of their own stories.
I once heard an acronym for HOPE, that it means
Hearing Other People's Stories.
One woman took time to write to me of the grace of recovery from illness,
and in another house, I hear from my own nephew
about what it is to get ready now for a parish trip
to a sister community in Central America.
that story, full of detailed courage and compassion. My own nephew.

A psychologist friend invites me at times to sit in on a group he conducts
with persons who are in recovery from mental illness, tough stories,

Selected Homilies

and one young man has recently been blessed with a visit
from a family member who had disowned him a few years back,
and who wants to find the way again into their being brothers,
into understanding, into forgiveness.
This happens to him, and is given, effortlessly to me in need of faith.
A brother seeking a brother for reconciliation.

Where do you need faith? What are you talking about along the road?

I remember reading once what Richard Rohr has to say about the crucified Jesus,
the sorrow and pain of this,
how important it is at Easter.
The cross with his body upon it, gazing at this, Rohr says
that it offers him at a deep level within himself
a compassionate view of God in life, in history
and I feel it coming to me
from my own friends: that compassion of God. Given to me too as I am.

And he adds that such a contemplative gaze might lead us to realize
that God participates in the suffering of human beings, of all creation —
not just God standing on the sidelines and watching
but God being with us in the suffering.

The contemplative gaze at the cross, at all suffering, that God is with us in this too.

I think that contemplative gaze might have opened up for Cleopas and his wife.
As they now and then stopped to breathe quietly. It happens as you
walk beside someone a half mile or longer maybe without talking,
to find what it means to know life given unexpectedly and so deeply.
How great a gift to be vigilant together. To trust your moment.
To discover the scripture stories, the length of our trial,
the persistence of all that goes wrong.

In the flow of life. Things gain perspective,
where our hearts are all at once burning.

Richard Bollman, SJ

So what are you talking about along the road?
"Stay with us, as the day ends, and the evening comes near."

And so he stayed with them.

The reference is to Fr. Richard Rohr's "The Mystery of the Cross" (April 23, 2017) at cac.org.

Christ hidden among us

Easter Sunday, B
Mark 16:1-8

On entering the tomb they saw a young man sitting on the right side, clothed in a white robe, and they were utterly amazed. He said to them, "Do not be amazed! You seek Jesus of Nazareth, the crucified. He has been raised; he is not here. Behold, the place where they laid him." (Mark 16:5-6)

HOMILY

Holy Thursday I went to visit my brother-in-law,
in assisted living at Twin Lakes. Lunch is the time to catch him,

with a few of his widower friends, at the end of the meal it was,
and I was introduced around, my name, their names, Xavier where I live,
the Jesuit thing, easy banter, a table of elders.
And shortly it was the two of us having a second cup of coffee,
when a woman from a corner table finished her lunch and came by.
She had heard all our intros, and had something on her mind.
A really pleasant woman, she was, a little younger than me,
and she put her hand on my shoulder so I'd look up at her.

"You're over there at Xavier?" Yes, I said, these last 30 years nearly.
"My son went to Xavier," she said. She needed me to know something.
"And he doesn't believe much any more. Just gave it up.
He says he's an atheist . . . . He's forgotten God." All this she said.
But somehow I didn't feel defensive, or guarded or even worried for her. There was
this smile on her face, and a lot of love for her son.
Let's say his name was Brian.
What she likes about him, even though he's an atheist,
is how good he is with his family, and extra commitments,
always doing for people. She was proud of him.
So I said, Well I guess God hasn't forgotten Brian.
Something I believe, and a way maybe to encourage her.

She didn't stay long, long enough for me to wonder
what Brian was like really. After she was gone, I wanted to continue
with my brother in law, what it might be like to have an atheist
at the family table on Easter. But his thoughts were elsewhere,
and I realized he could not hear our exchange, and had felt more embarrassed
by the interruption. But I liked it: I liked her affection for a son
who in some way troubled her, and I wondered how things would go for her
this weekend.

I thought if Brian had been with her he might have had his own word to say.
And I was just wondering what he does believe in, or not,
and what he thinks of his mother's concerns, if at all.
These are the quiet hidden themes at Easter, aren't they?
It's not that I wanted to evangelize her son.
Frankly, I wanted to talk about my own faith troubles at Easter time. Standing here in
front of you all, the empty tomb, "He is not here."

Richard Bollman, SJ

That empty tomb doesn't immediately encourage me in my faith life.
It's strange that Mark's Gospel ends right at that point,
and the women are more puzzled, more frightened than consoled.
I find myself saying, to the angel, "well okay. Now what?"
I find myself wondering, what do I believe?

Oddly enough, I think this is the right response to Easter.
A little bit of apprehension about what's next, and some wonder
about where Jesus is now, not in history but in my own life today,
This doesn't mean you've lost your faith.
It means you are more taken up with what I'd call the big questions.
About the real presence of Jesus, and his real absence too.
If anything needs to be noticed at Easter it is the first part of the message:
"He is not here." Not in the same way we think we should expect.

I have been reading a reflection about Easter faith by Krista Tippett.
You may know her public radio program, Speaking of Faith.
Easter certainly is a marvelous season, she notes, and we know how it goes,
but at the same time she tells us to notice the very strange accounts
of Jesus appearing to his friends after the resurrection, though they do not recognize
him. In those Gospels that tell about the women
after they leave the tomb, they suddenly and awkwardly encounter him,
hailing them down on the road. And Mary Magdalene,
who in another story looks into the tomb,
can't see Jesus when he's standing next to her.
It is mysterious how on the road to Emmaus he is not recognized,
and along the shores of the sea of Galilee the disciples don't recognize him
from the boat where they fish, not until he tells them how to get a good catch.

Ms. Tippett remarks that modern scholars frequently
put the details of the public life and the crucifixion under the microscope,
all about geography and teaching and discipleship,
but then after the resurrection, she is impressed more by what she calls
Christ being anonymously present to his friends in new ways,
new shapes, no different from the confusion he comes to help us to see.

Selected Homilies

So I feel less ashamed of my own confusing struggle to find him at Easter.
Christ has come exactly for this, to help me to see my own confusion,
to visit me in my darkness. And then of all things,
we come to see him at the place and moment of hospitality,
where love becomes practical, where we become closer to one another,
even aware of our wounds, as he shows us his, and asks for a piece of fish.

I wonder then if the woman I met, Brian's mother, is not herself
a kind of anonymous Christ, awakening me to my own questions,
even as she tells me of her love for her own son.
She offered me a sacred presence, the simplest eye contact
and a touch on the shoulder.
I think of her having Easter dinner with Brian,
and Christ anonymously and urgently present in their love.
And that is enough. Like the moment of breaking bread together at Emmaus,
Christ present even as he vanished from their sight.
And they remembered their hearts burning.

Here's what I know. The dear Christ we expect to find at Easter
may indeed be more elusive than we would like,
maybe interested more in transforming our faith
than in entertaining it in the old way.
That's what I know: we are not in charge,
and we are not cut off either.

And this too is what I know. We do what we can. We are here.
We read through the Gospel and learn he is risen, but he is not here;
But we are here.
We pay attention to an aging mother at Twin Lakes,
we allow for our confusion and maybe the kind of weak faith
that comes with having been church goers for too long;
and still we come. What else can we do, even if it's only once a year.

Because we have to be together, where hospitality happens,
where songs are sung and prayers are prayed.
None of this will bring Christ present as we expect him,

Richard Bollman, SJ

but all of it, even this morning, will help us stay awake,
so that when he does show up in our doubts and confusion,
we will be ready to see, and delighted to find him
with a hand on our shoulder and a smiling face looking with love into ours.

Alleluia. Amen.

Krista Tippett's book referenced above is *Speaking of Faith: Why Religion Matters—and How to Talk About It*

6. DISCIPLESHIP

Discipleship is a name for Christian spirituality. And Christian action. Let all of this come down to where we are, the day by day situation with its hopes, its openings to grace, and our slow learning. It is where Christ finds us unexpectedly, and where we find ourselves, especially among the poor or troubled or marginal. We are invited to be in solidarity, which can make us uneasy, but we don't back away. The Season of Ordinary Time.

martha's house

16th Sunday, C
Luke 10:38-42

Luke's Gospel is consciously arranged as a series of journeys. As you know, it begins with the journey to Bethlehem; then the family goes back to Nazareth but returns to Jerusalem for a visit. Then Jesus departs to the Jordan river and nearby desert, and a return to Galilee, a journey to the neighboring towns, and then deliberately to Jerusalem with his disciples.

Along the way, in Luke's Gospel, there are a series of important meals, places of refreshment, deeper contact with Jesus, usually places of special teaching, like the dinner at the house of Levi (Matthew), Simon, and of Zacchaeus. This dinner event occurs at the house of Martha. And her sister Mary is there too, (not Mary Magdalene). Some tension arises between the sisters about serving the dinner. But I want to first look at the larger context of the house and the occasion.

HOMILY

We read in other places about women who supported Jesus and the cause.
Martha may have been one of them.
She has her own house, so her family must have been influential.
A widow perhaps, or an unmarried daughter who inherited from her father.
It is hers, this house, the place where she is host.
Martha opens, invites, welcomes, receives:
and the guest is Jesus on a missionary journey.

No wonder Jesus could predict to his disciples
that there will be houses along the way, where persons of peace live,
and they will take you in.
Stay there accepting what is set before you.
If you read into the Acts of the Apostles, you find such houses mentioned there,
like the house of Lydia in Macedonia which welcomed Paul.
This is how Christianity began: not in temples or churches but in homes.

And those homes are a sign to us of what church is about,
I would think of them as safe places.
where people come to talk, to be helped, to be fed,
to pray together, to listen to the word of God.

Nothing has been more important to me through the years
than to support the safety of Christian community.
And to be a guest amid this kind of safety,
where you can sort out your thoughts, speak your mind.
People often find this in their parishes,
as has been the case here, I think, back through the years.
It has been wonderful to inherit such a house of Martha.
You can't just make it happen, but you encourage what seems to work.

But even so, working along with people and staff here,
sometimes my own worries or fatigue will dominate everything.

Selected Homilies

At your own home, you know this can happen too,
no matter how trusted the friends who surround you,
or how well things seem to be going on the outside,
you can feel the dilemma of Martha.
You get distracted in the work of producing something,
or protecting something, or making it right for others.

Like many a servant of God has said, surely through the years here,
"this is a lot of work, and I'm not sure anybody is helping me."
Just being the mother of the house, getting children up and out,
or preparing the readings or music for Mass,
or taking time for a meeting downtown some evening.
Church work, and we all do it, is often a lot of work.

I just want you to notice how the responsibilities of Martha
easily give rise to this kind of complaint: and you find it all around you,
in your school or office or kitchen, as well as in the sacristy of the chapel.
It is an important kind of moment because what is going on is this:
deep in the heart of the Christian servant
there is this desire to remember also to be a Christian disciple.
Underneath the complaint about needing help
lies a deeper question:
What am I in this for? How will I be fed?

The disciple is the woman or man who is hungry
for the word of God in Jesus, the word that is for you, for your heart.
It's an awkward place, this feeling of hunger,
and it comes up when we notice we're angry or envious of others:
that's one of the ways we awaken to a new kind of need.

The one thing needful.

Lately I've been feeling a great need for it,
wanting to hear the word: friendly and powerful and reassuring.
The one thing needful.

Richard Bollman, SJ

What are you carrying that needs the penetrating sound of that word
or song or touch that feeds you where you are really hungry.
The one thing needful.
Just remember, we are created, our bodies and spirits together,
we are made to be receptive to this word. That's a fact.

This word that will come to us–pay attention.
You might hear it in dozens of ways, in an embrace,
in the silent hope of a medical waiting room,
music you hear on the car radio, you might hear it in your garden.

We can avoid it, or get panicky that it's not meant for us.
Or we might be so used to just working and feeding people
that we never notice we're hungry too.
Or in my life I find that the brighter and safer you are,
the more interests you have,
the more you can avoid an important empty place
that longs to hear what God desires to say to you, give you, feed you with.
Just because TV or a late snack is so much easier.

Even so.
The more you allow yourself to recognize the need,
the closer you are to the feet of Jesus.
That may be enough.
Listening for the word of God is not like changing stations,
it's more like moving to another room in your own soul, a still place,
and it takes some courage, some getting used to.

So I recommend Martha as a model for us.
Let your complaint and misgivings be heard:
how about me, oh gracious God,
look at all this stuff I'm faced with: who's helping.

For a moment you feel unmasked:
you begin to notice your own envy and irritation and your anxiety,

Selected Homilies

your retreat into work to fill up what is lacking.
You find yourself exposed.
But at least you've said it.
"I want something more than all this effort."
You are entering the heart of discipleship.
And who knows what will happen next?

there will be enough

15th Sunday, A
Romans 8:18-23; Matthew 13:1-9

This is the first of the Parables in Matthew's collection. They are close to the heart of Jesus' way of teaching: stories about fields and pearls, baking bread, giving parties, and at the same time stories about God, about the presence and the power and goodness of God in all things, in the biggest picture possible. Sometimes the big picture turns our accustomed thinking upside down.

Accompanying today's parable about growing things is a section of Paul's letter to the Romans where the growth of our whole world, nature and the cosmos, is seen to be in an evolving struggle that requires great trust.

HOMILY

So here is Jesus approached by a crowd, responding to them.
His heart goes out to them, "like sheep without shepherds"
as Matthew reported earlier;
like human communities without a gathering place
or guidance to give them a better future.

His heart is inclusive:
People come because they feel welcome,
the marginal have some willingness to risk coming closer,
those who are 'sinners,' as we call them:
tax collectors, prostitutes, who else?
Those who wrestled with God, or with their families,
or with addictions. They would come in hope. We come too.

Jesus and the crowd, the great crowd. He has advantage and perspective
from the boat, across a little edge of water. So he taught them.
Not all of them were farmers, they weren't directly concerned about fields.
But it helps to know what fields were like in this culture:
they were surrounded by footpaths, it was a walking society;
the weeds from year to year were just dug up and turned under;
the sowing was not done in clear rows, but the seed was spread broadly
up to the rocky places. The fields contain the conditions of life and living.

So the crowd, and the fields, speak to the heart of Jesus.
Here is a parable with an exceptional turn of events,
a very satisfying harvest, enough grain to sell, grain for food,
more than enough. 100 fold, even, which is next to impossible!
60: a huge yield; 30 fold very very fine.
Even through the obstacles and uncertainties,
conditions contrary to growth,
there is a yield, there is enough. That's the turn of events.

You have to let this in, the sense of the parable,
that in the sight of Jesus our impossible or threatened situations
are not fruitless, not hopeless.
Yes there are disappointing parts.
Not every hope we have is fulfilled:
not every vision of a good life, or every hope for a good reputation
or a great job or a powerful place, it doesn't all happen.
Our particular hopes for a certain kind of Church;
or our favorite political program or candidate.
Not all of it will be fruitful.
Not every possibility within your children's graces and talents

Selected Homilies

will be received and welcomed by the world, and grown from.
There's a lot of waste, mistakes, disappointments.

But the main thing is, in the Kingdom that is God's,
there is precisely enough. Even more than enough.
Enough seeds find the moisture and good soil, and surrender their lives
so to change into something more, something of life.

Jesus trusts this. We need to look upon each other in the same way.
We see our mixed but essential humanity, and our wonder and our struggle,
and know that there is always within us
a tremendous goodness that wants to grow,
a cry of life itself to be let loose.
A sower went out to sow, a sower went out to that crucial place
of patience and work, where we find
God's steady and hidden graciousness.

I once read the account of a woman who took part
in a world peace conference
at The Hague, in the Netherlands. This was some years back.
Non-government agencies planned the conference;
more than 100 countries were represented, some 8 thousand people.
Such a crowd of people, 8 thousand stories.

She said something of this . . .
As horrible as the situation is in Kosovo and Serbia,
people shared stories of similar and horrible violence and genocide
in many countries . . . East Timor, Sri Lanka, The Sudan, India, Tibet,
among others . . . . people in this gathering, this world peace conference
shared their stories very freely,
and my heart broke, how could I respond?
only with tears.

And in the middle of the crowd, in the middle of these stories,
Archbishop Desmond Tutu spoke,

he spoke of the importance of nurturing youth
in their dreams and visions of a better world
visions of seeking the best for people,
learning to listen and find commonalities,
in a shared dream for life together,
learning to listen to and find common-life even in our opponents
rather than always seeking to highlight how we are different.

I think of that among our American young people,
or our young adult Catholics.
This word, in the midst of the stories. It was life reasserting itself.
But it had no particular plan or promise: it was sheer trust.

And, the woman said she also came away with a sense of being called
to recognize what she called women's work,
a work that comes from grief and from love for lost children,
where women work because they are the ones left alive,
mothers from Russia and Chechnya working together for peace.

She continued . . .
I left the conference bone-weary, completely drained
though more convinced than ever
the glimmer of hope among us in that gathering
that peacemakers will lead the way
toward a world where we know all our lives are immediately and intimately interconnected.

Like the archbishop, this woman too
found a capacity to look upon the crowd,
the human struggle of the world, and see a great possibility at work,
peace and interconnection.

Jesus tells a parable, calling that great crowd to listen deeply.
He tells the story of a field, and a sower.
It is a story of fulfillment:
of good ground, of a great yield.

This is not meant for comfort. The groaning of our planet can still be heard.
Parables are not meant to provide comfort.
They are meant to invite courage. And to re-engage us with the core of life.
They ask us to look again where our first glance might see only
loss and difficulty. Something else is also going on,
leading us to larger connections, a God more mysterious
and a God more close often than we like.

We need never be scandalized that some things don't work,
in our own life, or our efforts as a community.
We need to listen, keep our ears open,
to what God is bringing about, even as we wake or sleep.

getting closer to see

15th Sunday, C, 2016
Deuteronomy 30:9-14; Luke 10:25-37

Luke's Gospel is especially devoted to Jesus instructing the disciples. Our own ability to even hear what is said depends on our willingness to be disciples, open to learn the way, an open place in the soul. In this Gospel about the one we call the good Samaritan, we meet an aspect of ourselves perhaps, the inquirer who wants to know. And in that context, Jesus does not discuss ideas to tease us into thought, but rather he tells about real events, feelings, people.

Deuteronomy also, that teaching of Moses, stresses the same kind of truth about the way of God, that it is something very close to the human heart.

Richard Bollman, SJ

HOMILY

There is a kind of objective angle to the question: who then is my neighbor?
But instead of turning the lawyer's attention objectively to this world
of diverse communities, some of them friendly, some unfriendly,
some Jews, some gentiles, some Romans, Muslim or Arab,
all the ways you can sort people out . . . . that's set aside
and instead Jesus asks the lawyer to refer to himself, to come up against
that mystery: what kind of a man or woman am I? Am I a neighbor?
What can I know and feel and learn about this closeness to people?
It's patently an invitation to the listener to find yourself in the story.

It's a story about ourselves as disciples, willing to learn.
Am I able to look at a human situation, a person,
with my whole person, from my heart:
not dualistic: me and them, but wholistic:
I am like this person! That's the commandment, isn't it:
to love one's neighbor as oneself.

And so, in the face of an injured human being,
the Samaritan goes up to the person, goes close to see and understand.
And then a more whole exchange takes place. Mercy, Compassion,
the deep moving of the human heart.

This kind of response is what many of us missed
among some of the American bishops who negotiated the sex abuse crisis:
a failure to respond with the whole person, to go up to him or her.
A failure conditioned perhaps by certain needs to save one's reputation,
to protect the system from harm.
Like the priest: the law requires that he remain free from taint.
The Levite thinks: my role too requires a flawless reputation.
So you don't touch a dead body, you don't mess with blood.

I think of this too with regard to immigrants in our country
where frequently enough the distinctions, the questions we want to raise,

Selected Homilies

have to do with legality, illegality, documentation or no documentation,
and still, behind all this there is the struggle of the human person,
the tensions of North American economics,
and what is maybe a higher law: of mercy and compassion.
Christian teaching would want to defend
the right to find work where jobs actually exist.

You have to go up to the situation, what has happened to Mexico
since the free trade agreement changed the lives of farmers,
changed their small markets, made it difficult to gain a living.
I learned this once at a meeting about immigration in the archdiocese.
Current law is inadequate to the human need.
It's often impossible for example, that a native Guatemalan
can gain access to the US embassy to clear a migration journey.
And currently only 5000 such visas are granted a year.
While there are easily 100,000 each year to actually find jobs here.
Oddly enough, if they are deported they lose all;
the corporation who hires them loses maybe a thousand dollars.

Legal viewpoints don't get through to the human waste going on,
and the fear and family separations.
Good lawyers know this. Once you sort out the facts and the laws,
only then does the work begin where the human person
and human events become central.
What shall we weigh here? That is the abiding question.

I find this story intimidating: I'm not a man who likes to look closely
at the suffering of people, especially if I might take some hits
if I act or speak publicly in a way that calls attention to itself,
or breaks a taboo.

But there it is: the story where Jesus pushes the envelope a little bit,
and tells us what we don't want to know,
that being a neighbor is a way of life, not a behavior for once in a while.
Where the Christian way, the way of Jesus,
is caught up in our passionate self, our capacity to feel.

Richard Bollman, SJ

Go and do likewise? Maybe it means to get closer to where the wounds are,
to where your own wound is, your humanity, personhood,
and from that moment, you will find your path to neighborliness.
I do know, when I can respond,
it's often because I have borne the same burdens.
I know this place.

Or, another interpretation from my Jesuit friend Joe Bracken:
who believes that the Samaritan
is not the character who can show us ourselves.
We are the measurers and the passers-by, the ones who play safe.
It's just how human beings are made.
The amazing Good Samaritan is Christ.
He is the one, with the oil and wine and the lodging
and the offer to look in on us as long as we are in pain.
Just as he is the one who washes our feet at the table.
He cannot pass you by, will not.
It has been said, only God could be human as Jesus is human.

How does it go with you, when you have been hurt, left aside,
where you can get to a point of shame and not even want to be known there.
And yet it is exactly there in the vulnerable truth of being yourself
that you do deserve to be seen, understood, met with rescue and healing.
Completely undeserved except for the fact that, in all you suffer,
yes you are human, we are deserving, never unworthy.

Go and be likewise.

sent to be yourself

15th Sunday, B
Amos 7:12-15; Mark 6:7-13

Discipleship becomes a mission toward other people, our world now as we find it, as if there are some things we learn only when we are engaged and sent, only as we find out that yes, we can do something.

HOMILY

Here's what the Gospel says.
"They went out and preached that people should repent.
And they cast out many demons,
and anointed with oil many that were sick, and healed them."

That's what happened to them!
These are scary people.
You want to have them around, and yet you don't, maybe.
Something has gotten into them! And it does good for people.
Scary, in the sense of awesome.
Thank God they're here. Everyday you meet somebody or hear of it.
I know of people who lay on hands for healing, and it works.
I know of people who have been sent out, from this very room:
to Salvador, Namibia, Appalachia, young and old:
not many, but some,
going away from the secure place awhile to be present elsewhere.
I know of people who spend a day each week
washing the clothes of the homeless, while they shower and clean up.

Perhaps they don't preach repentance,
but their presence is a Word in itself, and it suggests that

Richard Bollman, SJ

change is possible, and that the truth of God is this:
we are together in all we go through. We can't just stand apart.
We have to see and touch and struggle with a new language
to be whole people in a whole planet. That IS repentance.
Always a little threatening, but it's where we need to be.

I remember when a friend of mine first got sober,
when his job was at stake and his mere physical safety was at stake,
and he dropped his hash pipe and martini in one move and went to an AA meeting.
He said at first it was frightening, the people there,
but then he just got a lot of life and courage from them,
and the demon began to leave.

If you'd ask, I guess I'd say I never saw a demon cast out,
and yet I have. There are these glimpses of how we encourage and
change each other.
My friend is steady and helpful to people now.
He had been about to leave the health-care business,
afraid he might be sued as a mal-practicing alcoholic.
Now he follows a private practice, counsels hospital workers,
and gives lectures on the spiritual care of the sick.

What got into him?
You could say, knowing the story, that the love of Christ got into him.
Or, like the sheep rancher Amos, God got hold of him, called him
away from his usual work, opened his eyes,
helped him to look and see what's going on,
and to tell God's truth about it.

Is God getting hold of you in any way?
I think that's the question we need to take away here today.
The prophet, woman or man, emerges, develops a whole new feel for life,
out of some brush with the sacred,
the Spirit waking her up, the shift in how the world looks.
It may be sudden or gradual. But it is a holy awakening.
It is the summons. You begin to get authority over unclean spirits.

Selected Homilies

You know what's right and what just can't be right.
You see the gaps in the social fabric even of our own prosperous world.

Amos, as an ordinary man of his time,
started to pay attention in the marketplace,
caught sight of the merchant's finger on the scale tilting the profit his way.
What would such a person do if he or she just opened their eyes
while passing through a contemporary mall.
What is happening around you in terms of sales and seduction,
profit and persons. What does it really cost to live well?
I was in conversation, a few years ago it was, but I remember it well.
Some of our young adult members were telling me
how hard it is to make good decisions in life, asking, probing,
how do you know when you're doing the right thing?
Well, I couldn't quite get the picture of their concern,
so I just did the uncouth thing and asked,
"Do you mean, like, about sex?"

"Oh no," they laughed and then turned very sober.
"No. We mean, what jobs are worth having,
how much money should you spend on yourself,
or on a house or car."

I had the feeling God was getting hold of them.
They were waking up to our culture, at least a corner of it.
They were on the brink of repentance: not
"I'm sorry, God, I'll do better."
But, "I want some good ground to stand on, new alignment,
a whole change of heart. I'm fed up with living as we take for granted,
where our heart feels nothing but the thrill of possessions
and personal relationships."

From little moments like that, some people have
wholly changed their professional aspirations and their relationship to the world.
As Amos said, "When the lion roars, who can help trembling?
When God speaks, who can help being a prophet?"

Richard Bollman, SJ

Is God getting hold of you in any way?
Have you ever been to one of those places in your own life,
where in the midst of what you're doing or needing or desiring,
somewhere across all the noise of our comfort zone,
you hear a lion roar? Just faintly?
The voice of God wanting to be heard.

Maybe it's just a notion like this:
"I have to change my mind about people who are different from me.
I'm sick of being limited by stereotypes and old prejudice."
Just an inkling!
Maybe it's just one final frustration about why our city
can finance stadiums while we limp along with low-income housing and
keeping good teachers. Maybe you ask that question once too often
and begin to follow where the question leads.
And you who were once a housekeeper and mower of lawns
hear the Lord taking you away into something new!
What's got into you, your children ask, your neighbors wonder.
"It's the lion roaring," you say.
Or, "I see God lowering a plumb line into my city.
How will we ever line up?"

Let me leave you with a moment from a good new book
called *Faith Works*, by Jim Wallis.
He writes about a parish that collectively wanted to do something
about youth violence in their area.
They needed more than talk, and more than theories.
So they invited, and somehow succeeded in getting
young people from the streets to come for an evening and talk.

And it led to a question from the congregation: What can we do?
And one of the kids said, "I dunno man, maybe you could figure out
what you do best and just use it."
And it led, Wallis says, to a kind of altar call: and people spoke up.
A college dean offered to take any of them on a campus tour and ask about
what it takes to join there; a cop and a drug enforcement officer asked
to meet with them to learn better what to do on the streets;

Selected Homilies

a pastor offered to open his church each afternoon for coffee
and conversation, and some business leaders talked about jobs.
And a woman who worked at McDonalds downtown talked about her break times,
and made an offer to welcome them for coffee and conversation.
"You know where to find me."

Wallis remarked after all this that he liked the offer from the last woman best,
because she understood what is essential in being sent out, or being available:
"Offering what you have and whatever you are, is enough."

what's on our plates?

> 26th Sunday, C
> Luke 16:19-31

"There was a rich man who dressed in purple garments and fine linen and dined sumptuously each day. And lying at his door was a poor man named Lazarus, covered with sores, who would gladly have eaten his fill of the scraps that fell from the rich man's table." (Luke 16:19-21a)

HOMILY

This is a story about the abyss that opens up between people,
people who should pay more attention to each other.
It's about what goes on nearby in our own neighborhood or home,
missing people because we are caught up with our own stuff.
Of course, the specifics in the story concern the rich and the poor,
the abyss that opens up between them: the abyss of class,
and of invisibility, that segregates a society.

Richard Bollman, SJ

But I think we understand that better
when we look at examples closer to home.
Because we all have our own way of being rich,
completely focused on the stuff in our calendar and among our projects.
We have a lot on our plate, as the saying goes,
and sometimes this leaves other people at the door,
left behind or neglected or unfed.

Let me describe for you an ordinary man, a father, a husband,
some man you might know with a lot on his plate.
Who can tell what pulls him into himself and his projects,
and so a gap opens up around him.
Imagine him to have a job in management,
looking for an advance in responsibility,
paying top attention to his department then,
and to the staff and assistants he's responsible for.
Imagine any two of those assistants, co-workers, putting up resistance,
nothing you can really nail down, but more an attitude,
but it makes the work hard and threatens his success,
and imagine the residue of that job crowding into the family room at night,
filling this man's attention with imagined strategies for the next day
but things he'd rather not talk about:
how this weighs upon relationships at home, or among his friends,
so he's always full of what seems important to him
but not aware of who else is around, hungry for his attention too.

You can't see all this inside a person,
since we take it for granted
that being busy and successful is the best way to live.
I remember knowing a man something like this,
who began to wake up, who lost his appetite for, as he said it,
all the crap he carries around inside.
He said that his children began to pull him out.
It's not an unusual story, but there he is, say,
with his oldest daughter going to junior high at Walnut for the first time.
His wife helped him see, perhaps,
to ask how much longer will he have a daughter
who really wants him to notice her, to walk through her math problems.

Selected Homilies

And so a man can push back from his own table
and find something more than the work there is to do.

Isn't this the heart of the teaching of Moses and the prophets
and the risen Jesus too,
Our life, our responsibility, extends beyond the table in front of us.
The calling is essentially this: begin to see who people are,
with whom we form a family, or a society,
see their real flesh and blood, their edgy places and their capacity to love,
because their well being is part of our own peace and integrity too.
Open your eyes to see, and then let yourself act, form new relationships.

It's great when this kind of respect for ordinary people
guides our social consciousness, the ministry of justice.
A woman in our own parish just sent an e-mail
that she would be away while
working with the Red Cross for the disaster victims in North Carolina.
It will be a hardship situation, she's been warned,
no electricity, not much water.
Okay, she is retired, yes, and so she can more easily
clear her plate and leave the table to help.
But what she models for me mostly is this desire to be there
to be part of healing and rebuilding
by doing what she can do.
I'm also impressed in the same way by local Cincinnati women
also from our own parish, who have helped to found Birthright.
Because their convictions about life
reached beyond just preventing abortion,
toward a desire to care for mothers and children both,
children who have not just the right to be born,
but the right to be wanted, fed, educated, housed.
I'm impressed with the imagination and action at work here,
toward the women who are up against our social system
in ways I do not see or know first hand.

Then last Friday I met another woman whose vision and action
remind me of this story of the rich man and Lazarus.
I took part in an afternoon tour of Evanston,

Richard Bollman, SJ

sponsored by Xavier's Community Building Collaborative.
The University has made connections to work in partnership locally
to help stabilize the commercial districts and to improve the housing too.
I found out Evanston is a strong community of home-owners,
more than 50% of the residents,
a larger percentage than in the city as a whole.
But it is vulnerable housing, vulnerable to being bought up for rentals,
which can weaken a community's sense of itself.
This was not a heroic trip, mind you:
but it did involve forgetting my own full plate for an afternoon.
So you get a feel for housing patterns, the rec center,
the struggle of small businesses,
and then unexpectedly, the key revelation was our visit to Hoffman School,
to listen to the principal talk, for just 15 minutes.

A young African American lady, she is, centered and present,
and the way she talked about the school showed such detailed knowledge,
for parents and teachers and students,
how everything is affected by the aging of the citizens, the home-owners,
the threat of old houses becoming rentals,
the fact that many of the school families are more transient
living in some of the least attractive apartment housing.

And she talked about the effort and hours she spends
following up with students,
less than 300 in all, calling homes, just to get them to come.
And she didn't blame any of these families.
They are just "kids raising kids," she pointed out, and they lack many models
of African Americans going to college.
Some of the partnership with Xavier
might be able to change this vision, challenge it.
Her voice conveyed such life and graciousness,
I find I remember a lot of what she said almost verbatim.
And here she was in a blue floral print maternity dress,
barely days from delivery. "Yes," she said, "they want to induce labor soon,
I'm overdue, but I think it's because I don't want to leave my teachers,
I don't want to lose track of the students:
what will happen when Mama is gone!"

Selected Homilies

Now this is a rich, well-educated woman,
not the first in her family who went to college,
who has pushed back from her own satisfied table
to work with the hungry, the struggling,
and with those so poor they don't know enough to want to succeed.
She is my image of God for this week anyway,
the God Jesus knew when he invented today's story.
She is like the lap of Abraham itself, all empathy and consolation,
and that is what God extends to each of us.
I'd like to work for her, I thought.

But maybe the real teaching is to pay attention to my own table,
and to call you to look up from yours.
What makes us happy, what opens the lap of God for us,
is to look up from our full plate, our projects and narrow vision,
to see the beggar at the door, the teen in our own house,
the students in our neighborhood schools,
pregnant moms who have lost hope, scattered people who have lost homes.

I am glad to pray here with so many of you, rich and not so rich,
who model this prophetic vision and action for me.

reaching past division

13th Sunday, A
Matthew 10:34-42

**Last Sunday we heard the middle part of Jesus' Missionary Sermon,
about setting aside fear and trusting God to be with you in your calling.
Today's concluding paragraphs group together some sayings**

Richard Bollman, SJ

**about loving Jesus and loving others in the mission,
about finding and about losing your life,
which are the personal struggles of the Christian walk.
And it ends with with encouragement about hospitality.**

HOMILY

Jesus talks about Christian life as a reaching toward relationships.
Especially with new people or strangers, how to yield time to know them.
Or when you are out of your comfort zone you wonder about your safety.
Or you might be challenged as you discover the suffering in people's lives,
and you wonder how to help, what to risk, how to be hospitable
but also to take care of yourself.

Jesus seems to be able to steer through all this stuff.
He had a wisdom about people and about his own heart.
He most often wanted to be inclusive and generous with people
And he passes that on to us.
In a simple way, he invites us not to fear people
but to see and feel their lives as your own.
Here are some events, memories, that make this real for me.

Back on a sabbatical trip in the nineties, on a short visit to Belfast,
I was picked up at the train station by an Irish Jesuit I'd met in the States,
and he showed me through the city by car,
the only time in seven months away that I felt anxious for my safety.
This was before some political resolutions, and open borders north and south.
And sure enough, we were stopped at a check point,
and Myles said to me, "Whatever you do don't talk,
don't even look interested; I'll talk. Only me."
Because, clearly, my American accent was a liability,
even and especially in the car of an Irish priest.
I could represent western interest in the IRA.
That was the last kind of attention the Jesuit group wanted there.

Selected Homilies

Actually what the Jesuits were doing there was a creative, personal work
to address the tensions and divisions in society in those years.
In short, they went to funerals. Like maybe here you would go
to the funeral of Mr. DuBose, or Michael Brown, where black lives matter.
The Jesuits had a small retreat house.
They invited people back to talk together, from both sides and all sides.
Grief softens hearts sometimes, and opens people to real experience.
Movement of spirit, ministry of reconciliation, could happen.
So there they desired to see the neighbor as one like yourself.
I felt safe spending the night there.

And here's a different story from Uganda.
Edwina Gately is a woman some of you have heard and read
and recommended to me. She is an English laywoman
and a church worker with a lot of faith and experience.
This is a story she tells, being on mission in Uganda
during the fascist reign of Idi Amin,
traveling with a priest by car to visit an outpost,
and they were stopped by a military roadblock,
a half dozen or so soldiers heavily armed.
She and the priest both feared the worst, abuse or rape, murder.
The soldier in charge lead her away from the car and across a field.
In a very simple way she found herself aware what was happening
and ready to die.

And then, she says,
from this moment of crisis all she could think to do was to
offer this man a cigarette. It was what she had.
But she had this overriding hope to meet him as a person. Amazing trust.
She said later that this offering shook the man deeply,
as if finally his own tribal customs came to the surface
and tore away the standards of violence and contempt he had been taught.
He accepted the gift, it was what his whole life told him to do;
and he wanted to give something back.
And he did, all he had, his gun.
And (this is so like her), she asked, "how does it work."

Richard Bollman, SJ

And he showed her, and they walked back to the car.
There were words of greeting and farewell,
and she as her companion drove away.

So at a certain point, something of being human
breaks through in the crisis. Our ego is no longer in charge.

Where does our love start to show up among the divisions of our world.
It's asking someone's name, offering what you have. A cup of water.
Once just in this past year I left the Taft theater downtown after a concert,
in the dark of winter, starting to walk fast, and I passed two big guys,
African American, at the corner there by the P&G colonnade,
and one of them opens a conversation with me, indistinct, and I thought,
oh what is this now. Well it was Grady Cook who I've known 20 years,
known mostly when he sells StreetVibes at our door,
and had to learn that I know him also on a street corner downtown.
I felt ashamed, I just said, well I hardly recognized you,
but really I had slipped into my ego behavior of separation.
But he was not separate, he was with life, he made contact.
He made it seem okay.

Barbara Fiand, a Cincinnati sister of Notre Dame, says this in a recent book.
"Everything that each of us does,
affects all the rest of us, directly and physically.
I am my brother or sister's keeper
because he or she is a part of me,
just as my hand is part of my body.
If I injure my hand, my whole body hurts,
and if I injure my consciousness – fill it with
malicious or selfish or evil thoughts – (fear, separation, e.g.)
I injure the whole field of human consciousness."

That is our calling. Not to do harm.
But to trust this possibility for change:
To see and feel the other as ourselves.
It is deeply human, almost intimate.
It is hospitality, love, losing your life to find it.

Selected Homilies

It is as near as your living room,
your office, your school corridor.
A cup of cold water.
You will not lose the reward of it.

Barbara Fiand, *In the Stillness You Will Know*, Crossroad Publishing, 2002, p. 58.

talking about love

6th Sunday of Easter, B
1 John 4:7-10; John 15:9-17

Here is a passage about discipleship, about the new commandment of love. It comes from the Gospel of John, given at the Last Supper, but meant also for the continuing and future life of those who assembled there with Jesus. It is an encouraging word about who we are, about relationship, mutuality in faith and trust. It is more than a command about behavior, it is the meaning of God and of life itself.

HOMILY

These words of Jesus are given at the supper table after dinner.
There was a certain urgency that evening. There was much talk.

Jesus had spoken of betrayal and departure,
he even spoke about death, without pressing the point overly much.

Richard Bollman, SJ

His friends were not ready to explore that topic too closely.
But mainly he spoke about love: and this is what mattered most to him.
The subject that night was love.
It must have felt wonderful to hear this kind of affirmation,
language of the heart,
even in a time of fear and uncertainty.

On Jesus' part, he had to unpack his heart because he had no time left,
and he was anguished and frightened of the violence ahead.
This makes things urgent for sure.
So the subject at the table was love,
something more important than merely living.
The subject was the value of each person,
each person chosen to be there, to be here.
The subject was joy, being fully alive, having a purpose in this world.

There was a mutuality in the room, growing trust,
and as Jesus spoke of love, these men, and who knows,
surely some of the women disciples with them,
felt a bond with each other.
Friends together and friends of the Lord.
This is that same table, you remember,
where as they sat down that night, Jesus had washed their feet, insisting
there is no ranking here, nobody is better than another,
nobody is superior.
This was a conversation among friends, friends aware of their faults surely,
but also friends who have come through a lot, and had grown up together.

Have you ever been there, at such a dinner, or on the porch,
or at a campfire, in the front seat of an automobile parked near a lake,
a conversation of friends, not a romantic connection, deeper than that,
and yet something that is felt in the blood and the heart.
It is like being grounded on the earth,
like being at home.
Maybe you never use the word love, because it is an overused word,
but love is there.
Maybe you never use the word God, because it too is an overused word,
but God is there.

I don't often talk about love, not even from up here,
but of course you have to bring it up at weddings.
There was a wedding yesterday,
and I enjoyed talking about love, about the marriage, about this young couple.
I felt in some important way it was a good marriage
even though the bride and groom are so different:
different churches even, Catholic and evangelical;
her Catholicism very explicit and full of ritual,
his faith so quiet, like a tree growing.
It was a pleasure to talk about it.
That's what I emphasized to the congregation, that in such a marriage,
the Church itself is becoming larger,
reaching out across old divisions, wanting to go forward now.
"You did not choose me, but I chose you for each other . . . ."
That is the spirit of their union.
So these things I spoke to them, and to their parents,
so that their joy might be full.
Sometimes it's like that, you just go ahead and talk about love.

Then last weekend I had the chance to meet three old friends,
we who lived through high school together.
It was our 50th reunion at St. Xavier, and you go
knowing you won't remember many, but ahead of time
the four of us determined we'd extend the party with lunch the next day.
We had not been together for 50 years.
One fellow's wife was recuperating from a knee injury:
he drove down from Detroit just for this lunch, just for two and a half hours.

We did not talk about love.
We hardly knew what we were talking about: some memories,
some grandchildren, some accounts of teachers,
at one point tracking down the biographical details we had missed:
graduate school, early jobs, a marriage, a divorce, adopted sons.
But I felt in tune with something I was glad to notice about my life,
something of its value and simplicity, something before any career
before my adult identity. It was like being somewhere, somewhere large and solid;

Richard Bollman, SJ

it was being someone graciously loved and important.
Is this then truly Christian faith, the revelation of Jesus to us?
Well, I do know the other three are all "still Catholic,"
if that makes the difference.
I can only figure out the meaning for me,
that I felt as if all my sins were being expiated
by the kindness of old friends.
I believe that the persons we were at eighteen
were living into our redemption,
we were abiding in life, with more joy and completeness than usual.
You know, sometimes you can see this happen at the lunch table.

The disciples at the Last Supper, they who were there and who remember,
what might it have been for them to have a 50-year reunion?
By that time, the temple in Jerusalem was destroyed,
but the city was standing open, subdued,
the old house of the supper table may have been standing,
or some inn or friends' home where they'd be welcome.
Some traditions tell that Matthew remained living in Judea,
so perhaps at his house they could come to eat.

Imagine Thomas come all the way back from India.
John, still very youthful at 70, has come down from Ephesus.
Barnabas, well known now, made his way easily from Antioch.
Mary Magdalene, a radiant 80 years old, in from Southern France.
Imagine the cries of recognition, the stories,
the way the suffering of later years only adds now to their delight
in seeing each other at the table,
each unpacking souvenirs, showing a scar or two,
explaining the customs and the food they've gotten used to.
All the lentils and basmati rice in Goa, the waving fields
of sunflowers and wheat that Magdalene found so healing.
There would be stories of martyrdoms, Peter's last days.
But the deeper subject of their reunion would be love,
that substance of God in which they have come to live.
They would talk of it without words, in the washing of feet,
in the breaking of the bread.

Selected Homilies

This is the love we are called to, by our baptism
by our communion in one another here in this chapel,
this inclusion, this hospitality,
the abiding presence of Jesus Christ in whom we live.
We have been given of God's own Spirit.
And we are all included: do not hang back.
Every memory and taste, the wine poured, the glances at the table,
all of it is clearly the remembered and real presence of the one
whose love was so great, he gave his life to bring us together forever.

the call worth trusting

Feast of St. Ignatius Loyola, July 31, 2011
Deuteronomy 30:11-14; Romans 8:35-39

For this command which I am giving you today is not too wondrous or remote for you. No, it is something very near to you, in your mouth and in your heart, to do it. (Deuteronomy 30:11, 14)

For I am convinced that neither death, nor life, nor angels, nor principalities, nor present things, nor future things, nor powers nor height, nor depth, nor any other creature will be able to separate us from the love of God in Christ Jesus our Lord. (Romans 8:38-39)

HOMILY

"Who shall separate us from the Love of Christ?" the apostle Paul asks.
And he enumerates his own struggle with life, with society,

Richard Bollman, SJ

with religion and with even himself! Tribulation? Peril? Nakedness?
Or the sword, or death, or life, angels or principalities?
Nothing, indeed, in all creation can separate us from that love of God
that is in Christ Jesus our Lord.

The apostle touches many a gentile heart
in a passage like this one, throwing himself so completely upon
Jesus, that presence never abandoning him in the midst
of all he went through, all his life demanded of him.
Where did this come from?

Confidence like that came directly from Jesus:
nobody taught it to him second hand.
He got it when Christ knocked him down, called him to change,
and then Christ began to tell him where to go, who to meet.
Paul compared his knowledge of Jesus, through this inner event,
with the practical experience all the 12 apostles had of Jesus.
He compares it to their encounter with Jesus risen from the dead.

Ignatius Loyola was also a man knocked down, made lame
by a musket shot in a local war between kingdoms of northern Spain.
And in his recovery, a painful and long ordeal,
he actually met Jesus through a book. Through a "Life of Christ."
He didn't have the Gospels, he had this extensive biography of Jesus,
one of the first written, by a Carthusian monk, something in print
because now there were printed books.
The monk, Ludolph of Saxony, wrote his Vita Christi
about 200 years before Ignatius read it.

At this point of convalescence, Ignatius was young, 30-ish,
hoping for a return to social life and prestige,
physical power, even some romantic love; though he also began to see
he'd limp forever, his youthful strength was fading,
his chances of political promotion not strong now.
And to pass the time, he had this book.
It wasn't the kind of book you just read from cover to cover:
it was a covert instruction in prayer.

Selected Homilies

It focused entirely on the humanity of Jesus,
and it charged the imagination of this man in recovery.
Ludolph wrote accounts of Gospel stories, all four Gospels
in a kind of harmonious chronology.
The idea was to read, yes, but to read so you remember
when the book is set aside. Remember it all, see it, let it rise up,
and then leave room for Christ himself to speak and act.
This began to touch Ignatius in his soul, in his feelings,
it revised his sense of what it might be to achieve anything in this world.
He found in Jesus, and some lives of the saints which he read
and contemplated in the same way, he found a model for living.
Here was a layman without any other plan to follow
except what Jesus was offering, as he met Jesus. He left home to follow it.

I point this out not just to introduce St. Ignatius to you.
But because really, this is very likely the way
many of us have met Jesus in our lives. Reading, remembering,
hearing the Gospel on Sunday, seeing a film,
seeing and feeling too, and coming to accept that Jesus is interested
in speaking within our own hearts,
capable of moving and acting and revealing himself.
And that's a life-changing moment. Jesus himself, intervening,
initiating something, joining you. Present, and human.

Here's a quote from the book Ignatius read, by this Carthusian monk
Ludolph of Saxony, with my own commentary in brackets.

"If you wish to be with Christ forever, begin to be with him now. . . .
Draw near to him who descends from the bosom of the Father into the Virgin's womb. Come forward with pure faith as another witness with the angel to his holy conception. Rejoice with the Virgin Mother who is made fruitful for your sake. Be present at his birth and circumcision as a good provider with Joseph.

[That's the special tone of it, that human engagement.]

Go with the Magi to Bethlehem . . . . Help his parents carry Jesus when they present him in the Temple.

[And there's a connection beyond words, feeling the weight and tenderness of a child in your arms.]

In company with the Apostles, follow the loving Shepherd about, as he performs remarkable miracles. Be present as he dies, sharing the sorrows of his Blessed Mother and John and consoling them; with devout curiosity touch and caress each wound of the Savior who died for you.

[Such a gesture! Straight from the world of medieval Catholicism and compelling as nothing else is. . . . devout curiosity!]

Search for the risen one with Mary Magdalen until you deserve to find him."

This invitation is what moved Ignatius to choose something new,
at this moment of being wounded, being willing, vulnerable to change.
Indeed, what is your own wound, your vulnerability? There it is,
as for Paul and Ignatius, where life stirs, where Christ is present and hopeful.
When you approach Jesus in this way yourself,
freely seeing and feeling and listening,
you find a place that becomes familiar and powerful for you,
where you can say all that you need to, bring all your regrets,
raise your complaints, express all that you love or long for.
It's not a book any longer, or a technique, but a place you come to know.
It's prayer in faith that requires very little word from us,
but the capacity to sense and trust that Jesus is moved by our presence,
and then to get a feel for what he might say to us,
to me, in this familiar place.

"Richard you've left a few things out today;
what is that dark bag of things
you hide in the closet and never show to me.
Let's just sit together and allow for more, just that.
It's what we both want. It's why I love you."
Does a person actually "hear" such words?
Why else might they flow easily from your heart?

Selected Homilies

So there it is, Christ strong and close to our own humanity,
and the humanity of Jesus with you, part of you.
You get to know it, and then things happen for good, for life.
I think this is how people are healed. And how we find a mission
worth following, people to love us, water for our thirst.
Such a place, once open, well you can always find it again.
Such a word, "very near to you, already in your mouths and in your hearts."
It's what we look for, we who search: the love of God
in the humanity of Christ Jesus, as Paul wrote long ago.

Trust what you know of it.
Trust what you've found of Christ.
And in that trust,
the next moment is already going to be shown to you.
Even today.

Quoted material above is a a small portion of Ludolph of Saxony's Vita Christi as published in *Studies in the Spirituality of Jesuits*, Spring 2011, p. 25. "The Prologue of Ludolph's Vita Christi," commentary and translation by Milton Walsh . . . recently expanded *Ludolph of Saxony, Carthusian. The Life of Jesus Christ, Part One.* Vol. 1, Chapters 1-40. Translated and Introduced by Milton T. Walsh. Collegeville, MN: Liturgical Press, 2018. Cistercian Studies Series: Two Hundred Sixty-Seven. With an editorial shift of diction: Ludoph says "reign with," not "be with" in the first quoted line.

7. END TIME

End Time is the name of that vast season far out and ahead, when the world will melt away, nations will be meaningless, and we will have lasting lives in a new place, God's own place, that heaven, that harmony. In the scriptures, such a speculation is described in beautiful physical terms, mountains and banquets and jeweled cities. Prophets held out such a hope, and so did several biblical accounts of the future, like the books of Enoch and Revelation. Jesus lived this kind of visionary faith; at least the Gospel writers have put such words in his mouth as he tried to reassure his own disciples in the face of his coming death. But it is finally death itself that defines such an ending, that which we all shall face, and so we need encouragement.

For it shall be a time of looking back and reckoning, saying Yes to what has been. It is the autumn of the liturgical year, celebrating the vast thousands of saints, and the dead with whom we still feel connected. And we come to terms also with the sheer mystery of dying to our bodies and our selves, what we have achieved, its value and its regrets. It is a season of trust at the brink of all we can ever know.

the nearness of God

30th Sunday, C
2 Timothy 4:6-8; Luke 18:9-14

He then addressed this parable to those who were convinced of their own righteousness and despised everyone else. (Luke 18:9)

Paul said to Timothy,
For I am already being poured out like a libation, and the time of my departure

is at hand. From now on the crown of righteousness awaits me, which the Lord, the just judge, will award to me on that day, and not only to me, but to all who have longed for his appearance. (2 Timothy 4: 6, 8)
Notes on the characters:

A PHARISEE was learned in the traditions of religious observance, eager to adapt and interpret them for his own time. Not all of them looked down on others, but you have to admit giving a lot of attention to observance of religious proprieties can lead in that direction.

The TAX COLLECTOR had the job of keeping the political structure humming by enforcing the tax obligations of the citizens. This being a Roman government, it was not a democratic process at all, and there was expectation for the collectors to increase their own rates in order to have some profit, while fulfilling what the government demanded. Whether wealthy, or just moderately successful, they had to endure a certain ostracism among their religious neighbors, since they worked for the system.

HOMILY

October starts to settle in deeply, the waning light, leaves falling.
I can only say there have been many extra gatherings here for funerals,
and it raises a kind of questioning in me:
like am I ready to die myself, I wonder?
It's not a bad question.

It turns a person toward a kind of inner look:
you check out your feelings, how you judge yourself,
what you've accomplished maybe, and a desire to open this up to God.
"Let's look at this together, God."
Think of this as listening in to the voice of your soul.

My soul's voice raises up some concerns about dying,
a sense of unreadiness.
I feel too much is unfinished, stuff I'd like to get better control of,

Richard Bollman, SJ

relationships I've kind of let slide.
And so I slip easily into the prayer, the soul-work, of the Pharisee.
It's a tendency to think we are living for the sake of achievement,
eliminating all our faults, ready to meet God with a great Amen,
that's what operates in the Pharisee's prayer, I think.

Is that what it comes to? I want someday to tell God I'm ready,
"I'm now totally transparent and honest about my conscience,
I no longer veg out surfing the web or eating the wrong things.
I have cleaned up my relationships, apologized correctly,
and think I'm virtuous enough to join the citizens of heaven."

"Boasting," is what this is called, in the parable we heard.
You probably know this side of yourselves too.
It's funny: we come to pray, to show up before God,
and we seem to be inventing the caption
under our high school graduate picture: "great guy, good musician,
fun at parties, always ready to go the extra mile with you."

Who would ever want to say we were:
"ignorant of our own heart, avoided responsibility,
self-indulgent, judgmental of others."
What would it be, like the tax collector in our parable,
to "humble yourself." The very word is repellent.

But essentially it means to know yourself as human,
to respect the human connections that surround you,
and to want a relationship with God that allows your whole self
to be part of it, nothing omitted.
It is a prayer that rises up from our worn spots,
the limits of what we can control.

We're invited to ponder the tax collector in the story
because he went home "justified," right with God, in tune with God's reign.
And I think his prayer is worth pondering
because in some essential way it is so much easier:
it comes honestly from "me the sinner."

Selected Homilies

What might have happened to bring him to this?
Maybe he caught a glimpse of the harm the system did to people,
and he was part of it. He saw the anxiety of a widow and her daughter,
deprived of safety and food because of the tax law.
"What a mess I'm in: God be merciful to me a sinner."

Or, say you're a junior in high school and routinely take part
in the kind of gossip and judgments that are normal
against girls who are overweight or guys who are nerds,
and you come upon someone who is convulsed in tears
from the things that keep her down and feeling alone,
and you realize how you've held yourself away from her
because after all you are so much more cool.
"What's going on here: can't this poor kid shape up . . . ."
A lot of our social world suggests that we evaluate ourselves
against standards that don't really suit, and that aren't very deep.
That's the source of bullying.
But then, a bully might wake up. "What's going on with me.
God be merciful, to me, the one I see in the mirror,
how clueless I am: Me a sinner."

So there you have it: two kinds of soul talk,
and one of them takes some effort, really,
to list your virtues and achievements,
and put all that out in front of you.
Such hard work. Is this what life is about?
And this kind of prayer seems to exclude the mercy of God,
that it's not needed, or perhaps not trusted.

Is this who God is?
I don't think God works to improve us according to our liking.
God simply pours out divine spirit, hospitably washing our feet,
in every moment old and new:
being redeemed and brought close again.
It's a mercy! to know how close God is to us, in our worn spots,
our addictions and irritations, eager to lift up those burdens
so we can enjoy our lives more.

Richard Bollman, SJ

In these days of autumn, when my own resources can feel worn thin,
and my compensatory behavior messy and off the charts,
these are the things that console my heart.
That the prayer of one's honest struggle is not too hard to find.
It's like Paul's prayer from the letter we heard:
we bring to it the miles we have traveled, the wounds we carry,
and our longing for God's appearing.

together in hope

November 2, All Souls Day
Isaiah 25:6-10; Romans 8:14-25; John 6:37-40

There is not much in the way of direct teaching about Purgatory in the Bible, but there is a good deal of vision concerning our passage to a new life after this one. We'll be drawing then upon three voices, three visions of where we are headed. One from Isaiah, one from St. Paul, one from Jesus. Each voice speaks in the prophetic tradition, where vision arises out of the needs of the present moment, to encourage faith during hard times.

HOMILY

I expect you arrive at this day with people on your mind,
the Holy Souls you remember intimately, their names, their presence.
Maybe you have written their names down, or heard them read.
Names, faces, friendship. They are not far.
We speak of the Communion of Saints: all of us,
earth and heaven and purgatory. Crowding in.

Selected Homilies

Isaiah tells us to imagine all the departed at a choice banquet:
that's where we shall be when the veil of our human life and death is lifted.
And the thrill of that for me is not so much the menu
but to have a place at the table. This is where Isaiah's vision satisfies,
simply to belong. Invited, known, sinners as we are.
God is full of hospitality. We have a sense of that even now. Enjoy it.
Hospitality, it's the context of God's mercy and vitality for us.

Just a week ago I spent two days with three friends
from my early Jesuit days: we are planning our 60th anniversary,
that's how long they have been in my life.
But we meet often even when there is nothing to plan.
The banquet is best when we just claim the kitchen table,
pulling up a chair or stool, breakfast cereal, fruit, a few eggs,
but mainly presence. Being there, being fully known. Having a place.
It is a kind of redemption, isn't it. All the broken parts of one another
are fully known, accepted, loved, even enjoyed.
Isaiah would recognize this table, and my joy at being there.
It is so close to us. The Communion of Saints.

Then let's appreciate the way St. Paul encourages his community
to trust God's powerful care in our present world.
I found a new poem by Mary Oliver who captures this well:
It is called "The World I Live In." The poet speaks of
how she abandons a house of reasonable proofs
and steps out into a world that is trustworthy, and wide.
As always, Oliver finds the truly salvific realm of God
is the realm of nature itself.

St. Paul's world was wide. He regarded all his communities
with feeling, with love and attention.
We are not cut off from one another, this world or the next.
A Communion of Saints wider than reason and proof.

Paul's vision of our shared future concerns
how it is taking place right now, in the pain of living,
the real things he lived with, dangerous travel, Roman prisons,
rejection by friends, narrow escapes, once over the city wall in a basket.
Paul must be one of the most optimistic humans who ever lived:
The glory and the struggle, they are so close together.
God is at work in the whole of it, like we are being born again.

My mother taught me especially on this day to reach out.
She went to Church to help release the Poor Souls.
It was a custom she had learned to care for old friends.
She believed that to make a visit to the church, on this very day,
to pray the Our Father, Hail Mary, and Glory Be, three times,
for a specific soul, this would release them already and thereupon!
One visit, which could be repeated in that same church
if you entered a new door.
St. Clement church, where she took me along for this devotion,
had five separate doors. I remember her serious purpose, reaching out
being in touch, people whose living and dying she knew well.

And so on this day of communion with the departed,
I take encouragement from Paul to go so far as to look across
our imperilled world, political and ecological, how it groans for release.
He encourages us to trust that God is at work in it,
beyond what we can manage.
Paul in those early church communities knew people's names,
and he knew the government forces large and small,
and he was at one with all who suffer. He believed
that the distress itself is a sign of God himself at work.
God's power is at work in our desires to be set free.
And that's what I learned from my mother: that yearning, that trust.

You don't have to look far to find that groaning, that longing for freedom.
We wake up with it each morning! If you are alive and conscious, there it is.
And so let's listen to Jesus Christ, a third voice in today's scripture.
Jesus declares that he has this one thing on his mind:
not to lose us. Not to lose us in death, not to abandon us in the present crisis,
but to bring us through.

Selected Homilies

This is our insistent faith, that Christ is with us in the hard parts,
Christ himself suffering and loving us in the groaning of the planet,
the loss of friends, the worry over illness,
the break up of homes, and homelands,
the crumbling of nation states, the threat of war or persecution.
He shares our human story, he invites trust and faith.
The Holy Souls know that now, deeply and intimately.

And we know it too: you feel it instinctively it as you read the paper.
We are reading about ourselves. As Pope Francis insists, don't turn away;
we belong together, we belong to this Earth, our homeland.

So I sum it up this way, the word to us this morning:
let us come to be ourselves, human beings in change and hope;
let us be citizens of this century willingly, fearlessly.
Remember to be stewards of this earth patiently.
Let it all be present today, in those you have lost, one soul at a time,
one tree leaf by leaf, one homeless family at a time, take it in,
let it speak and awaken our union with life everywhere.
It is God sharing our broken parts and unfinished hope,
breaking through our resistance, bringing us more closely to himself.
So much is dying, yes that is so. But then what is being born?
Even in you and me. That is our question and our hope.

paradise within

34th Sunday, C "Christ the King"
2 Samuel 5:1-3; Colossions 1:12-20; Luke 23:35-43

The history of Old Testament Kings stretches from 1000 years before Christ, beginning with Saul and David and Solomon, down to the end of the Kingdom

Richard Bollman, SJ

and the great deportation of the people, about 500 years before Jesus. After that, minor kings and tetrarchs ruled only with the permission of the occupying regime of Rome.

You can tell how important a person is by how rich are the stories kept about them. David was the first real success as King, and the stories about him are right up there with the Patriarchs, and the exceptional women of the tradition: Esther, Judith, Ruth. David combined the ability to listen to God and to make good political decisions. And he was popular for his personality, his military prowess, his skill in singing and dancing, even for his sinfulness and sorrow and contrition. So there grew up a deathless hope for another King like David.

Such hopes grew up around Jesus. But instead of a political revolution, Jesus prompted a revolution in consciousness, opening in everyone a new access to their own inner spirit, access to the reality of God. This was a power for self-knowledge, reconciliation and creative love, choosing everything from God's perspective. So would he even die rather than betray that truth.

HOMILY

Anyone who wants to know Jesus in a personal way
sooner or later will have to bring along their own cross.
Haven't you found that? No amount of "being good"
no amount of service work and performance wins awards in this journey,
but rather being yourself, exactly in your own limits,
and bringing also the injustices you've endured,
and the great hopes you have. And so you meet Jesus.

These things are often together within us,
an acute sense of our painful limits,
and a thirst for things to be different, new, more just:
for ourselves to be different, full of love and vitality.
All of it together is the cross we carry, the essence of our human condition.

Selected Homilies

As long as we think the cross is not important, or an embarrassment,
or a burden we keep trying to explain away or fix,
we tend then to hang back from Jesus, avoid his invitation.
But when we live with the cross and allow for it, accept it,
full of our sinfulness even, and our incapacity to save ourselves,
then our hopes have new life,
and our love has some way to express itself.

I think our search for God, as Christians,
is always going to be a journey of approach and avoidance
toward the humanity of Jesus,
until we recognize in him the inner light of our own existence:
how the cross, when it is understood and accepted,
opens us to an amazing place of being ourselves and being in God.

When Jesus was dying, such a conversion of consciousness took place
in a fellow human being on the cross, a fellow sufferer.
This criminal is the first example we have
of a person who literally carried his cross with Jesus.
Not just the cross of the world against him,
but of his actual existence,
a mixture of sin and hope, regrets, struggle.
In the presence of Jesus, in that shared dying,
he was able to acknowledge his own sins,
and still hope for something more.
And that was something beyond his abilities and skill.
In the midst of such an anguish, one human being to another,
he asked to be remembered. Just that.

Jesus' reply is worth pondering.
"This day you will be with me in Paradise," he said.
Paradise is not a kingdom. Paradise is a personal place,
the planted garden of a powerful home,
a royal park, a place reserved only for friends.
This is far different from gaining a pardon, or a reward,
or influence with the king.
Jesus says, in effect, Yes, I shall remember you,

and more than that, how would it be if I let you know
I love you in the midst of this death.
I love you for who you are
right here in the middle of what your life has been.
And I cannot forget you, because I have always been within you,
and this day you will be within me, and within that truth,
of your own goodness.
We will be friends, therefore, garden companions, always.
Beginning now, this moment.

This is what I mean then: this is a surrender
to the actuality of your own cross.
It is an approach to Jesus that overcomes all avoidance.
It is confessing your whole life,
and out of that self-recognition comes a desire to be remembered,
and an entry into an unexpected new place. Love alone.

I have learned about love by being witness to what happens
when a person comes close to death. Such a self-awareness takes place,
looking for presence, maybe reconciliation,
and there comes a new capacity to accept love,
to allow for it, from one's friends, your spouse,
the children coming together in the room.
It is not an easy moment, there may be nothing serene about it.
This is dying. And that's the point:
the cross stands visible. There is no hiding it.
Every fantasy about life falls away,
and so you can feel a kind of freedom coming close
in the midst of everything difficult.

I ask myself sometimes, what really have I experienced of love?
And when I peel away that need to compare myself or evaluate performance,
I think of what I have been witness to in the patience and endurance
of people committed to each other, together and yet separated in dying,
and so I have come closer to my own place of loving,
a capacity to be present and not turn away.
Love shows itself to us in the shadow of our own own cross,

and we can be drawn out to be patient,
seeing ourselves in everyone who dies,
and the word they give out,
however they say it, the word, "Remember me."

And right there, incredibly, is a doorway
into the garden of a more honest friendship with one's own soul,
a more hopeful existence.
Life becomes simpler.
The precious moment of each day, this moment we have now,
becomes "this day" when I'm invited to paradise.

That is what the kingship of Jesus is about.

in remembrance of her

34th Sunday, B "Christ the King"
Mark 14:3-9

In some lectionaries there is an alternate Gospel selection from Mark, about the Kingship of Jesus. Earlier in Holy Week he is a guest at the home of Simon the Leper in the village of Bethany. The disciples are with him there. And a woman came in with an alabaster jar of costly ointment, broke open the jar, and poured it on Jesus' head. She is scolded by some, for the waste, but Jesus has this to say:
"Let her alone. Why do you make trouble for her? She has done a good thing for me. Amen, I say to you, wherever the gospel is proclaimed to the whole world, what she has done will be told in memory of her." (Mark 14:6, 9)

Richard Bollman, SJ

HOMILY

"Anointing" is the word that comes to Jesus' mind
as the perfumed oil pours down his head, through his hair,
into his beard. Anointing makes a difference whenever it is performed,
blessing, healing, conferring a name or a position in the community.
Kings and Queens, you might say, are just ordinary people like the rest of us.
For their position and role they need to be anointed.
Elizabeth of England, in our own time, was anointed at her coronation.
And in the Hebrew scriptures, the Kings are anointed.
It is a way of making a person to be sacred, set apart.
It is a Spirit event too, an invocation that God's own power be poured out
so the royal leader can do what is beyond just human striving.
They are anointed to assure prosperity, win a victory over enemies,
achieving prominence in the world of nations.
Now this important gesture of anointing is usually done by a priest or prophet.
Not just anybody can anoint.

There is also a tradition of God anointing someone directly,
with the Spirit, with power and inspiration.
Isaiah speaks of himself this way, and Jesus takes it up from Isaiah:
"the Spirit of the Lord is upon me, the Lord has anointed me,
to bring Good News to the poor, liberty to captives."

Anointed: this is what the word "Messiah" means.
Peter the disciple acknowledged Jesus as Messiah,
"You are the anointed one we need," he said.

And then in the last week of his life, there is one woman who anoints Jesus,
who sees through to the essence of who he is, and who has to do something.
Jesus approves of her extravagance and kindness,
he takes it as a personal service.
He believes that she will be always remembered
by people who believe the Gospel.

This story raises two questions for me,
First of all, Who is this woman?
And then, How might we remember her?

Selected Homilies

Who is she? I feel sure she was one of his followers,
perhaps one of the wealthier ones
who supported him with her means.
The ointment, as everyone remarks, is expensive.
There is no hint that the woman is an interloper.
Here we are, she arrives while a meal is going on,
while men are with one another in conversation,
and her arrival itself does not anger the other guests.
I think they knew her: that is my guess. She is a disciple,
one of the group of believers.

But what gets to them is this gesture, the broken alabaster,
the oil running through Jesus' hair, and her touching him so intimately.
She stops all theological and political discussion that night. There she is!
They are amazed at her willingness to waste money on something so useless.
It's her joy, the love in her heart, that gets to them, not just the expense.
The expense is a dodge, a red herring.

And I think, underneath, they are embarrassed that she has got it right:
Jesus is the anointed one here, they are coming to see that;
he commands our affection and our generosity of spirit,
though his leadership is baffling.
At a dangerous point in his short career, in the holy city
well armed and guarded by Roman soldiers for the holiday season,
he suggests loving people we're taught to hate.
She seems to understand who he is. Jesus takes it as an anointing
on the brink of his death, as well as a declaration of royal dignity.
And this matters to Jesus, that he be accepted and befriended
for what he actually is, even if it takes our whole life to do this.

I wonder, later on, when word came to this woman that he had been arrested,
if she might have prayed deeply for him through the night of his imprisonment
thinking some fragrance of the nard ointment still lingered in his hair,
hoping her acceptance of him could be some help to him, saying
"I accept you, even in your dying, and I will come to be there."

Richard Bollman, SJ

Surely she did. She was one of those women
who did not turn away from the cross.

Now a second question: How can we remember this woman,
who points out the anointed Messiah to all of us.
We no longer have Jesus as a physical presence in town,
we cannot anoint his head.
We have only each other to celebrate, and the suffering, the poor
always with us. Is there some act of extravagance you've ever been drawn to,
some way of blessing and encouraging the human family we actually are.
I guess it could be helping a public school child to read,
or starting your Advent next week at a strange black Baptist church service,
with some other members of the parish.
Is there some boundary to cross, some holiness that cries out for recognition?
This must be what went through Mother Teresa's mind
as she first decided to lift up a dying beggar in the Calcutta streets.

Or, just look around this room toward the people
you find irritating or strange or out of it, and wonder,
is there some human spirit there within everyone
asking for praise, understanding, a gesture of anointing,
so God's spirit will shine in this way.
This kind of affirmation would release power and joy into this world.
"In remembrance of her, in remembrance of her, I will become this good news
for my imperfect world. I won't shrink back."

Maybe it's just sitting down with your close friends or family
looking at the great feast of Christmas ahead,
asking to know what it is we miss from each other at this season,
what single extravagant wasteful blessing we'd like to give to one another
instead of the list of obligations, expectations, ceremonies we don't need.
"In remembrance of her, I will become good news for my imperfect world.
I won't be always driven by lack of time, lack of resources, lack of faith.
I will break something precious,
feel something, do the good service, anoint and bless human beings
because we are the royal ones all of us, all through this royal city."

Selected Homilies

I think this is a way for the Spirit to break out of hiding,
through some generosity of spirit, some essential delightful giving.
There we encounter Christ present in this whole body
where he always lives. And then this even greater miracle can occur:
the Christ we thought was absent, or distant, or not relevant to our world,
Jesus as he is comes close, like the person next to us.
We touch his head.

the one we wait for

1st Sunday of Advent, C
Luke 21:25-28, 34-36

"There will be signs [. . . .] People will die of fright in anticipation of what is coming upon the world, for the powers of the heavens will be shaken. And then they will see the Son of Man coming in a cloud with power and great glory. But when these signs begin to happen, stand erect and raise your heads because your redemption is at hand." (Luke 21:25a, 26-28)

HOMILY

I've been wanting to understand what I am waiting for when I wait for Jesus.
Given the scripture here, I've been exploring what he says of himself:
that the "Son of Man will come in power."
You have to look around in the Bible, check the footnotes.
The term "son of Man" means simply a human exemplar, a human being.
Like a Son of the Old Sod, or a Daughter of New England,
a model of a certain type of person. Son of Man, a human being with a mission.
The term was first used by the prophet Daniel to represent an emissary
sent to reveal all that has been hidden. To sort things out.

Richard Bollman, SJ

Jesus uses this word of himself, Son of Man,
more than 70 times in the Gospels: in a variety of contexts.
Sometimes in calling himself the Son of Man he means one who is fully human,
and therefore capable of suffering, called to endure death, even to trust dying.
Son of Man, which is to say, one who is vulnerable and mortal.
The disciples understood what he meant, but resisted it,
the fact that Jesus, Son of Man, would suffer.

But also as Son of Man, an ordinary human being,
Jesus is willing to reach beyond human roles and limits.
When he does something which is properly godlike,
like when he forgives sin, gathers the outcasts.
These are things he clearly accomplishes in his humanity, as Son of Man.
But on a special mission.

And then at the end of his teaching, he raises the hopes of his disciples
that a time will come when all things will be sorted out
in the coming again of this Son of Man, all will be revealed.
This is the Advent meaning: sometimes this is called the Last Judgment,
but I'd rather call it the Final Revelation of who we all really are.

So it comes to this: in expecting Jesus the Son of Man,
I am expecting to encounter one who knows me through and through.
How does that sound to you? That great day of his Arrival.
It's always been a bit frightening to me, like, oh my God, I'll be exposed.
Do I believe that? But the point of this passage from Luke,
the arrival of Jesus, sorting out and gathering us together,
is an occasion to stand up and be counted, to raise our heads,
for our redemption, our ultimate happiness and liberation, it is happening.

So I've been allowing this to be true: that my deepest wish for Advent
is actually to meet up with Jesus as one who comes close to me
not to condemn or embarrass or judge me negatively. Maybe not to judge at all.
But rather to help me know myself a little better, deeply even,

Selected Homilies

to know myself as Christ knows me, as he loves and values me.
What would it be like for this coming of Christ to be close and affectionate
and a revelation of what God loves about each of us.
Would that take a lot of words? Would it be maybe more like an embrace?

I've been sorting photographs, so many have accumulated, from the parish here,
some from Jesuit reunions with my friends of 50 years, some from my family.
A few dozen have accumulated from my visits
to the East Asian Pastoral institute in Manila, all the ethnic dress and faces
from some 20 countries in that program I was involved with.
Interspersed with faces from baptisms and weddings,
from breakfasts in a vacation cabin,
and as I insert them in an album, they look back at me,
and I'm surprised how they all jostle together and move me again,
these different parts of my life.

I know the nostalgia I feel, the sense of loss and enduring love
is mixed with a wonder: because I show up in the pictures too.
And I say, who is that guy? Different poses, different ages.
What do I know of him, what do I remember and value.
I hope that I did not pass people by. Did they see my heart, and I missed it?
Oh that I had said a little more or hugged with greater appreciation,
I have been moved to write a few letters, to follow up with a phone call.
This is how it feels, this Last Judgment you might say,
the coming of the Son of Man, opening my own life to me.
Not saying much. Embracing me, I think. Redeeming all of it.

Where are your pictures, vacation files, reunion albums,
and how might you raise them up in the love of the Son of Man as he comes.
Waking you up to the living and the dead and the grace you have been given.
The days are coming, says the Lord, when I will fulfill
every promise I have made to you.

What a lift it would be to my spirits if I could allow the Son of Man
to be the best judge not only of my soul but of all souls.
To let him look at all the world's images and photos,

Richard Bollman, SJ

even where I shrink away or just get angry or fearful.
That would relieve me of the agitation and anxiety
by which I myself often become the judge of the living and dead, of everyone,
from the political debate platforms,
to the streets of Paris or Damascus, Washington or Teheran.
If I could just want to understand and open my heart and lighten my fears,
relax my arrogance or contempt.

In those days, says the Lord, I will not need to consult with you or the pollsters,
because I am one who creates and loves and raises up, and even laments,
it is mine to do, to know everyone in their ways according to the truth.
Oh to surrender to God the things that belong to God.

Behold, the Lord comes. The sooner the better.
Could it be, this Son of Man, who loves and understands and sorts out,
that he is here already, this Christ, who opens souls,
who exposes the righteous, the just and the unjust.
Is he perhaps not descending on a cloud, but stirring among the poor,
huddled with them in a stable or a train depot, on the steps of public buildings.
Could it be the poor already who point the way to what is right and what is wrong,
without rancor, without violence.
Who reveal the face of God, sons and daughters of humanity,
hard to mistake them.

It is with them, as Jeremiah foretold, that we shall finally dwell secure.
A restored people. And this shall be their name: "The Lord, our justice."
We shall all stand up to be counted.
Hearts and minds open to this very world and time.
Let it come, let it be.

Selected Homilies

8. THANKSGIVING

The bounty of God: this is how our Christian nation has explained our arrival and survival here in the new world. It is a story of conflicting values and injustice, along with evidence of God's providence and bounty. For this reason, homilies on this day try to acknowledge the nation and its native people, our debt to the past, along with the immediate recognition of the faith that sustains us, and the love that families recognize with one another. These pieces at the end of this collection continue to be meaningful to me, writing and remembering them.

a national story

THANKSGIVING DAY, 2011

HOMILY

Now that our national debate is focused on the economy,
stimulus packages, investment regulations, Wall Street, the national debt,
I feel pretty bewildered, not much able to take an informed side.
I miss the days of vivid, tangible issues, military intervention, civil rights.

On the other hand, I do certainly understand the stories
of lost jobs and under-employed friends, that's tangible enough:
families getting by on less, and the increasing gap of the rich and poor.
The New York Times covered yesterday the bleak end
of the congressional super-committee

and the chance that benefits for unemployment will evaporate.
So this Thanksgiving Day feels heavily burdened by these things.

So then you look back on this long tradition of communion and thanks
in our history: the great story of first harvests back in the 1640's.
That too is a complex and sorrowful story.
The account of the first Thanksgiving, written in a letter back to England, tells of an
assembly of more than 100 people, colonists and natives,
with fish and fowl and competitive games. I wonder:
What did they make of each other, the Puritans and the Pequots,
how did they talk of life and values,
how many little silent prayers were said that we'd make it through the winter
without some kind of cultural clash and disaster.
There were such different ideas about land, ownership, human rights.
It would be 50 years yet of raids and retaliations
before some kind of treaty was established, just in New England.

The American experience we've inherited
rests on early patterns of greed and exploitation
during those first 50 years of settlements.
Read about it in Howard Zinn's *A People's History of the United States*
how 10 million native people, in Haiti, the southern frontiers, New England,
10 million reduced to one million, through an exchange of diseases,
but more seriously from forceful control and casual massacres.
The colonial forces were interested not so much in the people they met,
who welcomed them at first,
but in the supposed wealth they could gain, even in native servitude,
for the sake of Europe. Spain, in those early days after Columbus.
And then England. The wealth taken back
only made the ruling classes more powerful,
allowing entry into wars that were often destabilizing on European soil,
and a devastation of the middle class peasantry.

Today's parallels are worrisome. Our war expenditures,
and the pinch against the middle class.
Well, so it goes, reading *The New York Times* yesterday.
Who will be gathering at your table today, with what anxiety or sorrow,

Selected Homilies

and not being able to much share it, because it is hard to understand,
and sometimes not welcome on a feast of thanks.
I wonder if this is not what motivates my family seeking solace in football:
the realities are tough in holiday time.

But then the *Times* also posted a column about thanksgiving itself,
about gratitude, which surprisingly helped me
come to terms a little better with this day.
Let me pass on what I can.

This article about gratitude, by writer John Tierney,
sorted out the benefit of gratitude as choice, a way of thriving really,
how it is linked to "sounder sleep," he writes,
"less anxiety . . . . and kinder behavior."
He helped me identify patterns of powerlessness and frustration
to be largely a trick of my imagination that can rob me of my own soul.

Gratitude, rather, is at heart the place of meeting God,
in what we call virtue, or true strength: it is an expression of
trust and hope. Giving thanks–and this was his best point--
is well beyond the social gesture of making someone feel good.
He points out that gratitude is not properly
an expression of indebtedness, where you have to be grateful
(that old prod parents sometimes use with their children:
"what do you say to Aunt Maud?" for her gift.)
Rather it is an act of vision, hope and depth in our communion
that reaches beyond our usual limits. Whether spoken or not,
It pulls people toward one another, and softens the stress
that leads to heart attacks, hoarding, or the need to prove yourself.
It partakes of transcendence.

I spent a good part of yesterday looking for moments of thanks,
as moments of vision, in the contribution of staff members
working those last hours before the break,
or the arrival of our cook at my community residence,
and the receptionist at the health center

Richard Bollman, SJ

where I spent an hour in the afternoon.
I'm sure they noticed nothing special in my dedicated gratitude,
but I noticed something lighter in my own heart, in my use of imagination,
like I was exploring the sacred tissue that truly does hold us together.
It's like grace becomes stronger than before.

"Thank you for being so careful of these wedding couples!"
I actually said that to Kathy. You know her: our assistant
for weddings and wedding preparation, a great solace
to brides and brides mothers. She was so dear as the day was ending,
taking extra time with a couple no one wanted to work with,
alums coming from the rough edges of Catholic parish life somewhere else. But
when I was exploring gratitude, her care became my own.
"Yes," she said, "they make unreal demands,
push boundaries and regulations,
but that's where I was when I got married,
on the edge of expecting anything of the church.
If I hadn't found an opening, I wouldn't be standing here today."
By mid-afternoon I had made an appointment with this ambitious groom!
to launch their marriage, because I saw that it would help a family,
maybe help the world.

It causes me to think back to a recent visit with my friend Jim,
who labors under the burden of Parkinson's disease.
People ask: how is he doing? And of course he is doing not a lot better,
with walking or standing or manipulating his motorized chair.
But I had to keep realizing how he seemed to me altogether more at peace
than six months back, more himself, more in the present moment.
And I think, in short, I was with a man more grateful for his life than before,
a gratitude that flowed over into my heart, about my life.
You come to see that no brokenness exists
that is not an entry into the care of a greater love.

The columnist in *The New York Times* quoted one Dr. McCullough, who says something very important about gratitude being the emotion of friendship, the feeling that helps you to realize that you are valued and matter more in the eyes of this person than you thought you did.

Selected Homilies

That is where I want to live. That is where you invite one another to live:
I've witnessed it so often, in times of joy and sorrow, that what matters
is the explicit notice we take of our own humanity, and how that is enough,
it is where Christ has found a home.
It is like standing in the wind of a storm, the heat of a furnace,
or the bedside of a newborn child:
for it is a great power that loves us even as it changes us.
May this richness find a home with you.

---

the article referenced is "A Serving of Gratitude May Save the Day" by John Tierney in *The New York Times* (Nov 21, 2011).

a personal story

THANKSGIVING DAY, 2006

HOMILY

A few days ago I was invited to give some thought
to what I'm thankful for these past few months.
You know the context: it was a small community meeting,
and the question could hardly be more open and innocent,
but I felt taken off guard.
Do you find this? There is something intimidating about
getting up your list of things to be thankful for.
I start to think very hard, and my mind goes into gridlock,
just trying to remember what has been happening at all,
trying to pare it down to the good stuff.

Richard Bollman, SJ

If you get like that yourself, I offer this reflection.
I find more access to my actual life by asking
what have I appreciated lately, (the shift in word helps me),
what have I been feeling, seeing, going through.
Don't worry about evaluating it or selecting a list.
Let the memories come.

The memories I wandered into, in the group sharing,
went along these lines:
a weekend in Chicago, a Friday night reunion
with a long-time friend and his wife out in a northwest suburb.
Call them John and Mary.
I needed to be in town for a meeting, and I called ahead.
The reunion visit fell together.
One of the Jesuits where I was staying near downtown
had no trouble driving me to Union Terminal,
this great old icon of a train station, the one with the flowing marble staircase
that turns up in gangster movies.

I hadn't been on a train in years,
and I boarded the northwest commuter train with time to spare,
chose a seat on the upper deck, read the *Chicago Sun-Times*,
and arrived out in Glenview at about 3:30.
John was there. We used to teach at the same high school.
He had been a Jesuit, the same entrance class as myself,
and married Mary some 40 years ago.
She was waiting in the car.
Most of their married years they've lived just two blocks from the train,
and John would commute grading papers through his long teaching career
at a junior college in Chicago's Loop.
They have two grown children, one of them a son who lives nearby.

But first John and Mary were willing to drive me out to Desplaines:
my request. I'd never seen the Jesuit graveyard for Chicago,
which occupies a separate plot in All Saints cemetery,

well beyond accessibility by the L train.
It was not cold, but chilly enough, a gray day, the plot of graves hard to find.
I remember getting in and out of the car half a dozen times.
When we found them, Mary was quiet, not knowing many of the departed.
while John and I walked among the headstones calling out names and stories.
Our teachers were there, the man who cracked our world open
with his course in scientific questions,
how the universe was really put together;
and another who brought us into the philosophy of the human person
by way of the questions being asked in the 60's by the existentialists.

We had to sweep the headstones clear of leaves: they were flat on the ground,
sometimes sunk below the grass. It was a search for no one in particular,
but then suddenly you'd find someone you forgot was there,
even a classmate who died of cancer back in 1990,
Gerry Grosh, some of you may know him:
he helped to found the Jesuit Renewal Center at Milford.
Appreciation was easy to feel, the stories were easy to remember,
and a kind of bond that still exists between me and a long-time friend
became more explicit, more detailed, atop these graves.

And then on the way back, as we approached Glenview
and I was thinking about a cocktail and dinner,
all we had planned and made reservations for,
Mary said: "oh look, Johnny's house, (that's the son),
it's right down this turn off.
Show Richard Johnny's house." So we turned.
The house was impressive in itself, settled in among a secluded cul-de-sac,
heavily wooded, all the lawns and leaves blending together,
the evening now bringing a glow to everything,
the yards and swing sets around, the suburban vans and bikes.
Neither John nor Mary expected their son to be home,
it was too early yet on a Friday,
but the large windows in their house showed activity in the family room,
and on a whim Mary said: "Richard's got to meet the grandchildren."

Minutes later, there we were, unannounced but welcome visitors
in the midst of a family quarrel. Joy, Johnny's wife and the mother

Richard Bollman, SJ

of their three children, was more than capable to handle things,
a kind of genius, an unflappable mom, part home maker,
part playground supervisor.
The two younger kids, Molly and Maeve,
screamed and tumbled toward their grandparents,
and we received word that Jack, the 5-year old, was himself on a time-out
from a temper tantrum, hidden away in his room upstairs.
Oh, a bad time to just drop in–"but this is Richard, John's friend,"
and then Mary would say deliberately to the children:
"he's a priest from Cincinnati,"
as I tried to imagine what relevance this would have to a four year old.
Even the angry oldest child got permission to come glumly down the stair
holding the bannister tightly as if to calm his nerves,
and greet me, and receive a kiss from his grandmother,
until finally in deference to their mother's
very different schedule and sense of the day
we got back into the car and drove away.
A short visit strangely perfect.

So there it is, a few hours in Chicago.
What had happened? Hardly anything, and yet like the events
of your lives here, yesterday, even this morning: quite a lot!
The course of living–it tells so much.
There was more for me: a good scotch, dinner, talk, photographs,
stories funny and sad, and as I told it a few days ago,
I saw how it lived with me. It has become a Thanksgiving Day story,
appreciating something of my own life through the years,
and something of the present day impact
of my friends' grandchildren upon them, John and Mary, and their retirement,
and all the undertow of living, the unexplainable,
the struggle within these events–
a young mother riding the waves of feeling in her home,
fielding the squabbles of her children, waiting for her husband;
the dead lying beneath the leaves and stones,
gone prematurely some of them,
or after illness, or suddenly at their desk, discovered one morning.

And within it all, my own desire
to realize the meaning of a 60 year relationship

Selected Homilies

looking to the past, tasting the pleasure of memories, shared names,
and then being silent witness to an unexpected turn
of the present moment for my friend John,
all he might have thought as Mary guided us down the cul-de-sac
to see their son's house, this impulse,
his pretty Irish wife of 1966 indelibly now a grandmother,
claiming this reality for herself, and wanting for me to know
the little ones she knows: Molly and Maeve and crabby Jack,
while John and I, her husband, savored our roots in classrooms.
Remember a scene like this for long enough, and you realize
love and friendship have so many faces, so much to experience and trust,
that you'd be hours telling somebody What You Are Thankful For.

So don't think so hard about it today: rather notice what you long for,
what you actually feel, what surprises you,
all that you really taste with those inside hungers,
for what life tells you, what love tells you.
Life as we live it has a mysterious sacramental power,
where what we go through yields its meanings.
This is the bread without cost. Transforming food.
As we taste it today and give thanks,
know that it is the table of the Lord's own supper with us,
and the table of our shared priesthood,
where we offer what we have lived, in spirit, in body, and in Christ.

Richard Bollman, SJ

Acknowledgments

My thanks to Brian Shircliff, founder and director of VITALITY, a center for yoga, healing touch and holistic learning. He designed a funding approach for the center, connected to books by his friends, privately published but available to everyone. I am grateful for him assisting this particular book with a year and a half or prodding, and finally with his advice and assurance.

We consulted then with Doug Klocke, professional graphic designer, who finished the cover and helped produce how the book comes across. He has been a member of the parish where these homilies first appeared, and a frequent collaborator there in design projects and promotion.

And my thanks to the parishioners of Bellarmine Chapel, at Xavier University, who have listened to all of these pages, or many of them, with comment and friendship and faith, starting back in 1992. I have expressed my thanks to them in greater detail through a homily given on the occasion of a 20th Anniversary Mass concluding my time as pastor. And that is what follows here, ending our book.

23rd Sunday, B
September 9, 2012
20th Anniversary Mass as Pastor,
Cintas Center Ballroom
Isaiah 35:4-7; Mark 7:31-37

Today's Gospel is a healing story, but it's not just a story of a man who gets well and can hear and talk. It's a direct fulfillment of the Prophetic expectations of the messiah, which is why we begin this morning with Isaiah.

The prophet speaks of the coming of God who is intent upon healing people and changing lives: exactly as Jesus shows himself able to do, opening our ears, helping us to speak and listen.

HOMILY

I need to tell you first of all I have always loved this job. It's gone through a lot of phases, it has not been easy every month, but it is wonderful to be welcomed in one's own home town and to be listened to, appreciated and loved, in work I like doing.

Amazing to think how we have been part of one another for 20 years. Thanks for being so free in your feedback, right from the start, not merely about what I might say on Sunday or in a letter, but about the general direction of the parish. Your responsiveness has made all the difference. It has helped me to know you, and to help the parish grow.

I'm looking here in this room at the life of the place: Friends in the Lord. A network of friends in faith, in ministry. It has always been a hope of mine that you would discover one another more and more graciously, and love one another even, in trust, in gratitude.

Sometimes at a parish meeting it would take me awhile to realize that the people in the room did not all know one another. I've always wanted to help that along. It takes time.

I think that friends who have faith easily become involved in listening–to one another, listening to life, and listening to the Gospel.

A parish especially provides a situation in which this takes place, openness to one another in what people believe and hear. Sometimes in the Gospel, like today, you see the story laid out: how in yearning to hear and to speak we are involved in a desire to be fully human. Something Jesus can touch.

Richard Bollman, SJ

As a former teacher of literature, I've grown up with the conviction that classic stories never lose their relevance, and should never bore people. The Gospels are at the very least classic stories like Chaucer or Shakespeare or Jane Austen for that matter. I believe that everybody walking in these pages is current, part of the present. I think that's the bias of St. Ignatius too, when he encourages a person to enter in to the Gospel and look around, to start talking, to pray. The Gospels are always going on in each of you.

The word is alive. Not every word, not every moment, but always something, some narrow opening to who you are, who we want to be. And what life is like. They show us ourselves in action, the Body of Christ.

In today's Gospel, I'm touched by the community's relationship with the deaf person: it's "the people" who bring the man forward. Who is this we all know and are concerned for?

I think of him as a teenager who doesn't have much of a voice yet, or maybe a widow whose grief has led to a silence, a distance, or someone alienated deeply, but someone that the people know and they long to assist this person, woman or man, and bring her to life. "The people," in this town new to Jesus, the people brought her forward.

The hearts of everyone are alert to such a person, and a prayer comes up. "Begging" that he would touch her, lay his hand upon the deaf one.

And then notice how it all needs a moment of privacy, an intimate contact. You do what you can, then Christ needs to act, to draw a person where they want to go. It's like the deaf man needed mostly a moment of silence with God, to feel that transforming presence and touch. To hear Christ groan.

Such a moment of encounter with a person who maybe can't hear or who doesn't know how to talk easily, but you take a risk. This happens, is happening in your homes, schoolrooms, the front seat of a car, being able to take someone aside in love, in concern, opening the ears of the beloved with a remedy of love and touch, never to embarrass anyone, but taking someone aside to let them know your faith,

Selected Homilies

letting your sigh reach heaven, saying, yes you can do it. So they come to know the precious core of their own truth, and begin to speak it plainly.

Isn't that the amazing part of the story. It's as if everyone has been concerned for this deaf man to finally hear what he has to say. What a moment of life and transformation.

I have seen these miracles, watching children I have baptized now take their place as teachers, catechists, lead singers, justice workers, medical interns. It takes caring and listening, transparent love. I've seen how your care for each other in the community draws people through grief, that deep silence, to new places of connection and prayer and trust. I've heard you say through the years how Bellarmine is a place of last hope, or a safe house where you can live your truth and find its purpose, tell its story. I'm glad you feel safe and received. It's not because of what I have sorted out or what the staff believes, but more because we share your need to find God's silence at times, and to move in the direction where Christ groans out a prayer for us all.

Friends in faith create a climate of consolation for the restless, the afflicted. Even up against the careless injustice frequently of the Church itself. Friends in faith can do this. Christ can do this. His groaning to God.

Now a few final remarks today. A woman new to the parish did me the favor of responding to a homily by quoting exactly what I had said, nearly verbatim, in an email letter. And even as I was tickled by that, I had to tell her that I was just passing on things I had heard from others. That what she had so carefully quoted was, well, not original.

I could tell her it was Pat McGrath, a younger Jesuit who had passed these words along in a Lenten talk here.

He said a kind of prayer, "God, suppose you would show me what it is that you love about me." I wrote it down that night. And passed it along last Sunday. I more or less take it that God is at work in these transmissions. And you can't always bring along the footnote. But the wisdom is out there, and it's in here, your mind and soul, when you recognize it. And then it becomes yours. Thanks be to God.

The woman said something else to me that I want to pass on: she said she was sorry she came to the parish so recently, and consequently so late in my time here. You know, I feel that too. Some members here, I think more than half, are indeed new, ten years, less, or only recently getting aboard, and I come to the end of 20 years thinking, "we're just getting started. If only there were more time."

And that's the main reason we come here as a full group today, the many of you who come, even some who are long long years here, but especially you who are recently joined in. We're here so you can look around and recognize the connections, that network of friends in the Lord, keep trusting this place. Trust your dignity as baptized Christians, invested in God's Spirit, even in a world of mixed truth and a Church of many sinners.

If only there were more time. But there is never any more time than the moment we are living now. It has to be enough. So you must say this to one another, what Isaiah said and still says, "you whose hearts are frightened, be strong, fear not, for here, at hand, among you, here is your God, the one Christ, alive with vindication and the power to free everyone." That's the divine revelation consistently and always.

Here I am. That's what God says. Here I am. That's why the stars exploded, the atoms fell into space, forming this green earth we can live upon. Here I am. And the blind see, even the deaf can listen. And we come to know ourselves as we are called to be under God's wing, in her lap, hand in hand with Jesus.

Selected Homilies

VITALITY
CINCINNATI

VITALITY began small, three of us at Healing Touch Program's Level 4 who dreamed about making Healing Touch affordable for all. Quickly, we gathered an important group of people from all walks of life who wanted to make that a reality. Self-care was very important to all of us — the 'good news' we wanted to share. We chose Healing Touch, yoga, journaling, meditation and recently added Movement Intelligence® & Feldenkrais Method® because they are all gentle, holistic modalities that can be learned easily and practiced by people in their own homes, with family and friends, often with very little equipment needed.

And that is how we work at VITALITY. Through these self-care modalities, we invite growth with one person who shares it with another person and another person, and before you know it, there is a holistically-minded person in every home in Cincinnati, Northern Kentucky, and all over the world who can share what they know and listen to and learn from one another's experiences.

In a most important sense, then, it's relationship that is vital. Perhaps these 'modalities' are simply ways of opening to one another, of being fully alive to one another . . . to see and hear and sense the wholeness — THE ALL — of one another.

VITALITY was founded in 2010 as a 501(c)3 charitable/educational organization. We rent a small space in Norwood, the center of Cincinnati. All of our programs welcome everyone and are donation-based . . . from a handful of change to a check.

Since beginning VITALITY's Yoga/Healing Touch Internship — which certifies 200-hour yoga teachers — our graduates have shared yoga and Healing Touch-inspired meditations all over the country — even as far as South Africa!

Our Yoga/Healing Touch Intern-Graduates have shared their gifts in college yoga clubs, among high school faculty/staff, in recreation centers and gyms among all ages, in fields, at traditional yoga studios owned by themselves or friends, at businesses and research labs, in garden centers, in restaurants and tea houses, in parks, in food pantries, in churches and places of worship, in coffee shops, in community rooms, in food courts, in senior centers, in board rooms, in art galleries, among grade school & junior high faculty/staff, on farms, in barns, in fields, in prisons, in hospitals, in health centers, at resorts, in factories, in centers for the blind, in their own homes, in apartment community rooms, in recovery centers, at farmers markets, at breweries and bourbon distilleries, at food co-ops, at pre-schools, at orphanages, at homeless shelters, for hospital networks, in classrooms, at cancer recovery centers, in auditoria, at nature centers, in garages, in grocery stores . . . in just about any place you could imagine.

And what's even better, these graduates create their own brands, their own versions of moving-breathing-resting that are not VITALITY's brand. Graduates create small businesses to help themselves and their families thrive holistically and financially by meeting their class-participants where they are.

Some graduates share their holistic-gifts for a living, as full-time or part-time jobs; others volunteer as they are able; others share with family and friends as they feel most comfortable. Nearly all of our graduates offer at least some classes by donation (as we do at VITALITY) or on a sliding-scale.

One day, VITALITY hopes to have its own energy-self-sufficient building, retreat-house, and publishing center that will gather funds not only to keep VITALITY Cincinnati growing but will also provide seed-money & micro-lending for graduates and groups of people like VITALITY around the world committed to deepening the growth of humanity on this planet through:

organic community gardening and healthy-eating gatherings where relationship and ideas are born;

Selected Homilies

places for the study of gentle movement, meditation, contemplation, nonviolence's cleverness . . . where people gather to imagine a new world, a citizenship of the world-over where we recognize our planetary intraconnectedness . . . where we might cleverly, nonviolently, joyfully, freely, responsibly, and abundantly live together on our earth for many more generations as we discover and live out our common human life together;

small communities that use earth-friendly energy-sources and seek the joy of self-sufficiency, minding the relationships between and among all that lives.

We welcome you to join us and share your gifts, especially the most important gift of your presence.

vitalitycincinnati.org

VITALITY

buzz & books
(re)discovering roots
vitalitycincinnati.org

available through vitalitycincinnati.org, Amazon, and your local bookstore!

A New Setting of the Spiritual Exercises: Hearing, Seeing, Feeling Old Stories in New Ways
(2015, 2nd Edition coming in 2019)

Brian J. Shircliff offers a very different take on Ignatius' notebooks that gave birth to Ignatian Spirituality through the Spiritual Exercises, and yet this 'new setting' is very true to the spirit of Ignatius. Authors Dan Price, Tamilla Cordeiro, Brian Geeding, Maureen Sullivan-Mahoney, Bridget Rice, Mike Eck, Carol T. Yeazell, Shelia Barnes, Theresa Popelar, Richard Bollman SJ, Bailey Dixon, Melanie Moon, Jalisa Holifield, and Elizabeth J. Winters Waite contribute their personal lifestories to the book . . . the book's true richness. An interview with Jean Marie Stross, Dan Price, and Richard Bollman SJ offers a context to this new setting of the Exercises, part of a larger re-imagining of the Exercises in Cincinnati and around the world.

Sweet Lady J...Mother, Muse & Root of Nearly Everything: The 3000-year-old Campfire Stories of Biblical Genesis Giving Birth to Judaism, Christianity, Islam, Nonviolence & Neuroplasticity (2017)

With an original and lively translation from the Hebrew text into English, Brian J. Shircliff takes us on a journey into the first strand of the Bible.

Coming in 2019 . . .

yoga is THE ALL: an invitation to <u>sensation</u>al life's authors Brian J. Shircliff & the Companions of VITALITY Cincinnati offer questions, experiences, stories, brief histories, quandaries and more about the 3000 - 5000 year very permeable history of yoga. They invite us to wonder about what yoga was like there in the Indus River Valley long before the shapes (asanas) had names, before there were instructions on how to breathe or meditate, before their were ayurvedic prescriptions on what to eat and how to live based on people's types, long before yoga became a $16 billion+ industry in the United States. Through their diverse, personal experiences, the authors invite the notion that yoga can be for ALL to better know THE ALL.

The Naked Path of Prophet . . . Brian J. Shircliff offers a new translation of the Bible's 1 Samuel with invitations to the prophetic ecstatic-visionary-healing lifestyle of Jesus, of many

CPSIA information can be obtained
at www.ICGtesting.com
Printed in the USA
FFHW020537060919
54785701-60455FF